# GRANDMA
## AND
# GRANDPA CAMP

*Inspiring Stories to Strengthen Generational Bonds*

MICHAEL AND ROSEMARY GREENE

Grandma and Grandpa Camp: Inspiring Stories to Strengthen Generational Bonds / by Michael and Rosemary Greene

ISBN: 979-8-89694-528-4 - eBook
ISBN: 979-8-89694-529-1 - Paperback
ISBN: 979-8-89694-530-7 - Hardcover

Forward by: Debbie "Nana" Mrazek

*To our children and grandchildren who continue to brighten our lives with laughter and love.*

# CONTENTS

# FOREWORD

Needing to grab lunch between sessions at a conference, I saw a lady I had known for years through the technology industry. You know how girls do: "Hey girl, want to join me?"

Rosemary was a technology business owner I admired, who I had known through community events for years. Seldom, though, had we had a one-on-one conversation about anything other than our industry and businesses.

This was a women's conference we were attending, so talking about business and other things seemed quite okay. When I asked her what she had been up to outside of work, her eyes lit up like a child does when you mention Santa, and she said with a lilt in her voice, "We just finished Grandma and Grandpa Camp!"

Well, of course I had no clue what Grandma and Grandpa Camp was, but she seemed so excited that I had to ask, "What is that?"

Oh, my heavens! She proceeded to tell me how once a year, she and her husband, Michael, get all their grandchildren together—*without their parents*—and the only rule is that they have to be out of diapers to attend!

To say I was intrigued, delighted, and 'tell me more' excited would be an understatement. She was absolutely infectious with her joy, speaking of this event.

She went on to share *how* it worked! They gather all the children for a week, make a super fun plan for things to do (parents are not part of this planning process) and go about with great fanfare and joy doing it. Every year is documented in pictures and words to cherish for always and to share with grandchildren who are not here yet.

As time went on and the grandchildren got older, there was never a time that I did not ask about Grandma and Grandpa Camp. The stories were always grand and got grander when the kids got older to give more input on the plans.

A few years ago, when I asked about it, she shared that that year, several of them were older and teenagers, so they thought they would not want to do it anymore. To take the pressure off, they told them directly that it was okay if they no longer wanted to participate because they had other things they were interested in now.

I wish I could have been a mouse. To the kids, I guess it sounded like maybe they didn't want them to come, which could not have been further from the truth. They *all* still wanted to come, and to this day, *they still do.*

A couple of years ago, I had the pleasure of being in Rosemary and Michael's home for a holiday gathering with *all* of these grandchildren I had heard about for years. From the outside looking in, it was magical seeing the bonds and experiences they had created and how they evolved to do other things with *everyone* included, like this gathering. They had shared in the planning, preparing, hosting, enjoying, and celebration of the moment.

Can you imagine your grandchildren wanting to be with *you* and only you, *every* year?

Fast forward from when I first learned about this incredible idea. I had children who were teenagers, a long way from being parents. Today, I have two beautiful grandchildren of my own and you guessed it … *yes!* We have Grandma and Grandpa Camp every year at our house. They are young, but I see this beautiful tradition growing and enriching our lives over the years, as it has for Rosemary and Michael.

What an extraordinary legacy to leave our children, grandchildren, and great-grandchildren. This "How To" Manual will be the most priceless of any you have ever used.

Happy Grandparenting!

Debbie "Nana" Mrazek

*Debbie Mrazek is president of The Sales Company, a Texas-based firm that helps hundreds of entrepreneurs, individuals, and corporations better assess, understand, and engage in practical, purposeful selling. She has counseled, constructed, and created sales programs, workshops, and individual and team coaching. Debbie is also a speaker, author, and conference facilitator.*

*In her best role, Debbie is also the proud grandmother—aka Nana—of Hazel and Wilder and has her own version of Grandma and Grandpa Camp—Nana and Pop Camp!*

# INTRODUCTION

Some of our most cherished memories are when we spent time with our grandparents one-on-one. One of my favorite memories is from when I was a little girl, going with my sister to Grandma's house to color Easter eggs every year for our younger brothers and sister.

How often have you heard friends say, "If I had known how much fun grandchildren would be, I would have had them first!"

Have you ever met a grandparent who does not have a picture or pictures of their grandchildren with them in a wallet, a purse, or on their cell phone? They will proudly share these pictures with their friends, colleagues, or even a friendly stranger at the drop of a hat. We admit that we can be counted among this group of proud grandparents.

We are a couple who value family relationships. As a result, many family traditions have developed, including what we call Grandma and Grandpa Camp. Later, you will learn how we came up with that name.

**Make a splash**

Our family consists of four grown children, their spouses, and eight granddaughters. Yes, all girls. The two oldest granddaughters have graduated from college and left the nest. Three are in college now, two are in high school, and our youngest granddaughter is in middle school. There are seventeen years between the oldest and youngest granddaughters. Like many families, our children live both near and far from our home.

Over the years, we have been privileged to have all our grandchildren participate in Grandma and Grandpa Camp.

Every summer since 1998, we have chosen a week for Grandma and Grandpa Camp. During this week, we gather as many of our grandchildren in our home as can come. Over the years, the number of campers has ranged from as few as two to as many as six. We take a week off from work to devote our time to them.

During camp week, we share many adventures, some at home, some away, some planned, and some unplanned, but we always enjoy the time we spend with each other. We share interesting things, learn about what they like to do, and provide opportunities for learning and exploring together. But most importantly, it is just time to be together.

We have experienced such joy because of the memories and close relationships we developed with our granddaughters and the strong bonds they have created with each other.

During this time, as we talked with friends about our week with our granddaughters, many expressed enthusiasm about the idea. Some have already started their own version of Grandma and Grandpa Camp. Their excitement about this idea encouraged us to write this book.

In this book, we share some of our adventures with our granddaughters over the years. You will find examples of planning tools and ways to find adventures to share with your grandchildren at home, in the neighborhood, and in your community. Most importantly, you'll see the impact our Grandma and Grandpa Camp has had on our relationship with our granddaughters.

We hope that by sharing our story, you can take some of these ideas and create special memories with your grandchildren.

# CHAPTER 1

# WHAT IS GRANDMA AND GRANDPA CAMP

---

Each year, we look forward to having our grandchildren join us for a week in the summer, where we share hugs and stories and make memories together.

It's hard to explain the delight when our granddaughters join us each year at Grandma and Grandpa Camp. We learn about what is happening in their lives and continue strengthening our relationship with each of them.

Unlike family gatherings where we only have a few hours together, the extended time at Grandma and Grandpa Camp allows us and the girls to get to know each other well. As a result, the cousins have grown close and have become best friends. They continue to stay in touch by texting one another often.

For one week, two to six of the eight cousins come together under one roof to share two bedrooms and a Jack-and-Jill bathroom. Can you imagine six young girls sharing one bathroom?

Whether playing in our backyard, going on a picnic, visiting a museum, or doing other things that have become our favorite adventures, Grandma and Grandpa Camp is all about shared experiences with our granddaughters, building strong relationships and precious memories.

Every year, the anticipation builds as our granddaughters eagerly await the start of Grandma and Grandpa Camp. They can't wait to spend time with us and each other, creating a sense of joy and excitement that fills the air.

While we put together a schedule of activities and outings for the week with input from our granddaughters, "downtime" is an essential part of our schedule. Free time at home allows the girls to share their creativity with us. It is also a time for playing games, telling stories, and sharing what is happening in their lives.

## How It Started

With the birth of our first grandchild, Ashley, we began to know the joy of being grandparents. Like many grandparents in this new role, we saw the kids and their parents as often as possible—on weekends, holidays, birthdays, and any chance we could!

After the birth of our second granddaughter, Lindsey, we had the opportunity to have both girls in our home for a week while our daughter and son-in-law went on vacation. Ashley was three, and her sister Lindsey was a year old and still in diapers.

We scheduled the week off from work and began planning their time with us.

**Day outing**

Our time together flew by as we played in the pool, went on outings, visited the park, went for ice cream, played games, took naps (for both the girls and us), and read bedtime stories. This was a special time for us and the girls.

When the girls went home at the end of the week, they told their parents what a good time they had and wanted to come to Grandma and Grandpa Camp again next year. Grandma and Grandpa Camp was born.

This is also about when we realized why God rested on the seventh day. He was exhausted!

As time went on, cousins joined in the fun. Our group grew from two to four to six granddaughters spending the week with us. Breakfast outside on the patio, a morning splashing in the pool, working on a puzzle, coloring, or working on crafts at the kitchen table were just some of the ways we shared time together.

**Cousins joined the fun**

After the girls washed up and prepared for bed at the end of each day, Grandma would read them a bedtime story. One of their favorites was *Make Way for Ducklings,* by Robert McCloskey.

The story takes place in the Boston Public Garden, where you will find a pond with a small island just perfect for Mr. and Mrs. Mallard to make their home for their eight ducklings, Jack, Kack, Lack, Mack, Nack, Ouack, Pack, and Quack. Over time, as the number of campers grew from two to four to six, each of our granddaughters chose one of the ducklings as their alter ego so they could become part of the story.

The adventure takes Mrs. Mallard and her eight ducklings to meet Mr. Mallard on the island in the park. On their way, they must cross a busy highway and side streets. With the help of a friendly policeman named Michael, Mrs. Mallard, with her ducklings and our granddaughters, made the harrowing trip to their new home safely.

Today, there's a sculpture of Mrs. Mallard and her eight ducklings making their way to the island, displayed in the Boston Public Garden.

## Rules for Grandma and Grandpa Camp

Like all families, we have rules to follow when we are together. Grandma and Grandpa Camp has only three rules that are not very complicated.

Rule #1: No parents allowed. Grandma and Grandpa Camp only begins when the last parent has left the driveway. Our granddaughters take this rule very seriously. The following stories demonstrate just how seriously the girls feel about it.

Our granddaughters and their mother from Austin arrive at our home Friday evening before Grandma and Grandpa Camp starts. Their mother stays the night and returns home on Saturday morning. At an early camp, Lindsey, who was three then, came out of the bedroom on Saturday morning eager to start day one at Grandma and Grandpa Camp. Surprisingly, she spotted her mom sitting at the breakfast table, having coffee and visiting with Grandma. She immediately began to cry. Her mother picked her up and, giving her a loving hug, reminded her that she loved coming to Grandma and Grandpa Camp and would be fine. In reply, Lindsey sobbed, "But that's not the problem. You're still here!"

A few years later, the number of campers had grown to six. In 2016, Grandma and Grandpa Camp was scheduled for the first week of July. That year, the 4th of July fell on Monday, day three of Grandma and Grandpa Camp. The parents from Austin stayed over the weekend to celebrate the 4th of July with the rest of our family in the Dallas area. The girls complained that they got short changed three days that year. They reminded us that rule #1 says no parents allowed. That year, Camp started on *day four* in their minds.

Rule #2: Swimming every day. Because we have a pool in the backyard, this rule is a no-brainer. However, last year, we decided to fix the cracks in the deck surrounding the pool and, while we were at it, resurfaced the pool, too. While watching the workers jackhammer the deck and replaster the pool was fun, swimming in the backyard was not an option that year. One of our neighbors offered to share their pool with us. We made it work with that and a day's trip to a water park. It wasn't the same, but it worked out okay.

**Swimming with Grandma**

Rule #3: Have fun. We never have trouble having fun at Grandma and Grandpa Camp. Rain or shine, we are in it together. As the girls grow older and more cousins are added, the desire to spend time together creating memories and building lasting friendships continues. We can't wait to see what's next. Who will be able to come next year?

As you can see, our rules are pretty simple: no parents allowed, swimming every day, and have fun. When you decide on your rules, make them simple and positive, like having fun every day. Perhaps there is another activity they will enjoy doing every day besides swimming. Keep the number of rules to a minimum.

In addition to the rules, we remind them of other guidelines for being considerate of others. For example, make sure things are picked up so there are no tripping hazards for Grandpa.

## Mealtimes at Grandma and Grandpa Camp

Mealtimes are a great time to talk with your grandchildren about anything and everything. They love to hear about your childhood. Where did you grow up? What was life like back then? They also enjoy hearing what their parents were like when they were growing up.

**Mealtime together**

Meals are also a good time to listen to what is going on in their lives. What are they excited about? What do they do for fun? Who are their heroes? Mealtimes are filled with storytelling, laughter, talking over one another, and sharing life experiences, both yours and theirs.

It is a time to let your hair down and enjoy getting to know your grandchildren better. This is where bonding begins and continues to grow.

## Win, Win, Win!

One day at lunch, we talked to the girls about writing a book about Grandma and Grandpa Camp. They were so excited about that idea that they immediately started listing topics that we should include. We mentioned that a definite topic to include is how camp is such a win, win, win! They were puzzled by this topic and wondered what it meant.

So, we explained, "You love coming to camp, right?"

The response was a resounding "Yes!"

That is the first win!

"And we love having you, right?"

Again, a resounding "Yes!" The second win!

"And your parents love having a week to themselves, right? Right?"

A puzzled look was on their faces. That thought had not occurred to them, and they weren't sure if it was true. From conversations with their parents, we know that they enjoy the time to work on projects, have date nights, and be together as a couple. A third win!

## First Timers

As the number of campers grew, we added a requirement that campers be out of diapers before coming to Grandma and Grandpa Camp. That just made it easier for us. You can imagine the time involved in changing diapers for multiple campers.

Just like beginning school, every granddaughter has a first time at Camp. First-timers include not only the grandchildren but also their parents. This may be the first time their child has been away from them for an extended period, and they miss having their little one around.

When Ainsley was able to come to camp the first time, our daughter and son-in-law, who live nearby, were missing their daughter and dropped in mid-week for a quick visit to get a hug and see how she was doing. She told them all about the fun she was having, gave them hugs, and went back to playing with her cousins.

With the second child, things are different. The parents are excited when their child can join the fun at Grandma and Grandpa Camp, and they can enjoy their week of date nights. They also put much effort into potty training so their children can come.

## As They Grow Older

Once our granddaughters started high school, we thought they would be too busy with band camp and summer jobs to continue coming to Grandma and Grandpa Camp. But we were wrong! They continued to join us each year, all through high school, even though for some of them it was now just a Grandma and Grandpa Camp weekend.

When the youngest cousins were able to come in person for the first time, it was important to the older ones, who no longer could spend the entire week at Grandma and Grandpa camp, to join them even for a short time, so that they could share their camp experiences with their younger cousins. That year, we had six girls with us for the weekend. That included three college students who made the time to be with their younger cousins at our home.

**Older cousins welcome first timers**

As our grandchildren move on to college, our close relationship with them has been established, and we want to be a part of their college life. During conversations with them, we find a weekend that works around their activities, exams, and other school events so that the two of us can visit them at their school for a weekend.

We get a personal tour of their campus, see their dorm room, meet their friends, visit some of their favorite eating spots, and hang out for a while.

So far, we have visited the University of Illinois, Purdue University, the University of Texas, the University of Alabama, and the University of South Carolina.

We have been a part of their lives as they have grown up, including attending their graduations from grade school, high school, and even college. We have already attended two weddings and expect to share more memorable moments with them as they grow into adulthood.

*****

So, what is Grandma and Grandpa Camp? It can be a day, a weekend, or a week. It is about spending quality time with your grandchildren, getting to know them as individuals, and sharing your life with them. The results are absolutely amazing!

# Chapter 2

# Fun Adventures at Home

When the girls were preschool age, playing at home in the pool, getting a push in the airplane swing hanging from the tree in our backyard, all the while laughing and yelling, "Higher! Higher!", taking afternoon naps all together and reading bedtime stories at the end of the day were simple things we could do at home.

The following are some of the activities that were big hits for our granddaughters. We share these stories to spark your imagination about some of the activities you can do in your home with your grandchildren. Remember, not everything you try will be a big hit, but don't let that stop you.

**Airplane swing**

## The Toy Chest

Like most grandparents, when our first grandchild was born, we immediately searched for things for her to play with when she visited with her parents. In no time, we had a collection of stuffed animals, noise-making push toys, a Fisher Price Doll House, a Farm, a Garage, a Medieval Castle, and other toys we picked up from garage sales in the neighborhood.

15

Over time, we continued to add to our collection of toys, which now fill a closet in the second bedroom.

What will your Toy Chest look like? Will it include a slot car racetrack? Matchbox cars? Legos? What are some of the toys your grandchildren will enjoy while at your home?

## The Dress-Up Trunk

We had the winning bid for a dress-up trunk at a church bazaar that included boas, children's plastic high-heel shoes, a poodle skirt, pop beads, assorted dress-up jewelry, stylish hats, purses, and even a pair of angel wings—it was a church bazaar after all. Grandma added her own assortment of high heels, dresses, and jewelry to expand the collection.

The girls loved playing dress-up, combining boas, high heels, and assorted accessories to create their very own fashion statements. Then, they presented their fashion show, waving their arms, flaring their skirts, and twirling their way across our living room.

Dress-up

Most toddlers love to play pretend. Playing a superhero, doctor, truck driver, chef, cowboy, a ballerina, nurse, princess, or some larger-than-life character. The dress-up trunk is the place where your grandchildren can find their costumes. Once they have changed into their favorite character, stand back and join them in their imaginary journey.

## Pop-up Playhouse

We found a pop-up playhouse on the internet that could be set up in the front hall or backyard in seconds. This playhouse had a door that opened in the front and a window in the back to let in light and fresh air. To add a touch of excitement, there was also a secret escape portal on one side.

Add a couple of small plastic chairs and a small table, and you have a playhouse that took almost no time to build.

So, what is this playhouse? Is it a fort? A castle? A hideout? It is whatever your grandchildren decide it should be. The possibilities are endless.

## Backyard Fun

Get outside! Find yard games that are great for all ages. Horseshoes, Croquet, Badminton, Bocce Ball, Corn Hole, or playing catch gets you out of the house and into the action with your grandchildren.

Outdoors is also a great place for doing things that would create a mess inside. One year, when our granddaughters were grade school age and older, we decided to tie-dye t-shirts. It's a fun project, but definitely an outdoor activity.

A backyard picnic is always fun. It can be breakfast, lunch, dinner, or snack time. Throw down a blanket or two and add sandwiches, chips, and a favorite drink to get the ball rolling.

**Tie-dying**

If you have an outdoor grill or fire pit, roasting marshmallows on a stick and making s'mores is always a big hit.

Because we have a pool in our backyard, we also looked for pool toys that our granddaughters could enjoy. The pool store has many toys for grandparents to share with their grandchildren.

**Grandparents' boat**

In our case, we purchased the "Grandparents" boat because, as we were told by the clerk at the pool store, no parent would spend the money to buy such a toy for their own children.

We also had a small red plastic slide about two feet tall that the girls would put at the pool's edge to add a water park attraction to our pool.

Another favorite pool toy is the Volcano, which, when inflated, is an island in the pool that they can swim to and sit in as it floats.

**Volcano**

While the "Grandparents" boat and plastic slide are long gone, the Volcano is still a major attraction at Grandma and Grandpa Camp.

## Murder Mystery Dinner

One special activity is the Murder Mystery Dinner, which is one of the highlights of Grandma and Grandpa Camp. We search the internet to find just the right murder mystery.

**Grandma did it!**

Once we have the script, each camper is assigned a character and given their part. At this point, no one knows the identity of the guilty party.

The girls raid Grandma's closet and the dress-up trunk to select just the right outfit for their character. Once the dinner starts, we each follow the script, doing our part to offer clues and answer questions from the group.

As the dinner progresses, more clues are revealed, until it is time to vote to see who we think is guilty of the murder and why we think so.

Some things seem too obvious, and it is easy to jump to the wrong conclusion. Like a jury deliberation, we all discuss the clues we have uncovered and look for the strongest motive before finally deciding on the guilty party.

While we don't always get it right the first time, the person "Who Done It" is revealed in the end. Last year, it was Grandma!

*****

**Activities at home don't have to be complicated. Sharing time with your grandchildren can be as simple as playing a game, reading a story, or having a picnic lunch in the backyard. The time you spend together creates memories that will last a lifetime.**

# CHAPTER 3

# EXCITING ADVENTURES
# AWAY FROM HOME

---

In addition to the fun activities at home, we look for opportunities in our community to share with our granddaughters.

Our area has many adventures to explore, including museums, miniature golf, laser tag, parks, scavenger hunts, and more. The following are some of the experiences we have included in our Grandma and Grandpa Camp over the years.

## Fossil Hunting

We packed a picnic lunch and headed to our neighborhood park with our granddaughters, where the girls could run, play tag, swing, or climb on the playscape to their hearts' content.

There is a shallow stream cutting through our little neighborhood park. Along its banks, we had a unique opportunity to hike with the girls and explore the treasures contained in the banks along the stream.

As they walked along the banks, they made some amazing discoveries. They found many impressions of fossils in the clay—impressions of leaves, shells, and ancient fish. One impression of a fish was the length of our granddaughter's forearm!

**Fossil hunt**

Our budding paleontologists were looking at impressions of fossils from more than 260 million years ago when the state of Texas was almost completely underwater. How cool is that?

Don't have fossils in a park in your neighborhood? How about a scavenger hunt? Neighborhood parks are full of surprises.

## Larger than Life Sculpture

Pioneer Plaza, located near Dallas City Hall, is the home of a larger-than-life bronze artwork. It is a re-creation of a cattle drive celebrating the trails that brought settlers to Dallas.

The site includes a waterfall, man-made cliffs, native plant life, three cowboys on horseback, and a herd of forty longhorn steers.

The girls enjoyed running (little ones never walk) around the cliffs, stopping to admire the cowboys and swinging on the horns of longhorn steers.

**Playing amoung the longhorns**

Google "Outdoor Art Near Me." You may be surprised by what you find.

Visiting outdoor sculpture sites is a great way to harness the seemingly endless energy of the young.

## Awesome Day Trips

**And we're off**

Sometimes, we want to spend an entire day away from home to visit a special place. Places like Dinosaur Valley State Park, where our granddaughters were able to stand in the footprints left by dinosaurs over 113 million years ago. It is one thing to read about dinosaurs in a book, but it's a totally different experience to actually stand in one of their footprints.

Fossil Rim Wildlife Center, where the animals roam freely in the park, is another up-close and personal experience with nature. We drive through the park and can feed the animals from the safety of our car.

Day-long outings are fun, and sometimes, they can provide unexpected adventures.

## Train to Fort Worth

On one such trip, we took the train from Grapevine to Fort Worth.

**Train to Fort Worth**

We arrived at the Grapevine Train Station to purchase our tickets to the Stockyards Station, located in the heart of the Stockyards National Historic District in Fort Worth.

We boarded the train and found a seat in an authentic 1920s Victorian-style open-air coach. A red 1953 GP-7 diesel locomotive named Vinny pulled the coaches. We were transported back to the time when train travel was in its glory days as the nation expanded west.

It was a sunny summer day as we pulled away from the station, and the wind was in our faces because large openings lined each side of the coach instead of windows as we started our hour-long journey to "Cow Town."

As part of the entertainment along the way, the train was "held up" by Mustang and his gang of outlaws. As the train moved along the tracks toward Fort Worth, the gang of bandits galloped up on horseback to the train, shooting their six guns in the air and demanding that the train come to a stop.

Once the train stopped, the bandits boarded and proceeded with the "hold up." Of course, these were not real bandits. Instead of demanding our money, the desperados handed out play money to the passengers.

Shortly after the bandits boarded the train, the sheriff, Deputy Maverick, showed up and asked for volunteers to be his deputies to track down the outlaws and protect him in case a gunfight broke out.

Ultimately, the bandits got away to "hold up" this train again another day, and we continued on our way to Stockyard Station.

## The Old Chisholm Trail

We visited Cow Town in Fort Worth to stroll along Exchange Avenue, where we could explore the Chisholm Trail.

The Chisholm Trail was used in the post-Civil War era to drive cattle overland from ranches in Texas to Kansas. Cattle drives started in the Rio Grande area or San Antonio and continued through Texas and the Oklahoma Territory to the railhead in Kansas. From there, the cattle were sold and shipped eastward.

**Cattle drive**

We got to Fort Worth in time to see the Cattle Drive. It was like we were back in the old west where the cowboys and cowgirls on horseback moved herds of longhorns from behind the Livestock Exchange Building down Exchange Avenue in the Stockyards National Historic District.

These longhorn steers can weigh between 1,400 and 2,500 pounds each, and their signature horns measure six to ten feet, tip to tip.

This was a fun adventure—the girls could talk with cowboys and cowgirls on horseback and pet their horses. However, they were disappointed because they expected the cattle drive to be a stampede!

After the cattle drive, it was time for lunch at the Mexican restaurant next to the Stockyard Station. After a lunch of tacos and chips, there was still time to check out the shops nearby and pick up souvenirs to remember our trip to Cow Town. This included getting cowboy hats for the cousins from out of state.

## Exchange Avenue

There is always something happening on Exchange Avenue. During one visit, the girls participated in a fake cow milking contest. Each girl took a turn to see who could get the most milk from the cow in 60 seconds. There were many laughs, and it was definitely a first for our city girls.

On another trip to Cow Town, we encountered a group of players dressed as the sheriff, town folk, and an Indian. We were transported back to the 1800s in the Wild West.

But there was still more excitement to come. While we could not call this a "Bull Ride" at the rodeo, our youngest granddaughters, Story and Colette, did get to saddle up on a real live bull.

**Bull riding**

## Cowgirl Museum

Given that we have eight granddaughters, a trip to the National Cowgirl Museum and Hall of Fame is a no-brainer. The collections in the museum document the history of pioneer women from the Old West to the cowgirls of today.

**Cowgirl Museum**

Annie Oakley, Dale Evans, Georgia O'Keefe, Patsy Cline, Laura Ingalls Wilder, and Sandra Day O'Connor are among the more than 250 Hall of Fame honorees in the collection.

In addition to the numerous exhibits, including fancy dresses, boots, and saddles, there were interactive exhibits where the girls could digitally design their own cowgirl shirts, skirts, or boots.

They could test their riding skills by saddling up on a mechanical bronco and be featured in a real rodeo video clip to be downloaded when we got home to share with family and friends.

You may not have a cowgirl museum in your area, but you should have a county or state fair. Fairs are a great way to connect with life outside the city. Livestock exhibits, horse shows, and a pig race are just part of the fun. There might be carnival rides, and don't forget the food. Corn dogs are a hit with every fairgoer. A day at the fair will be a cherished memory.

## Frontiers of Flight Museum

How cool is it to have a personal guided tour of the Frontiers of Flight Museum by the captain of the Zeppelin airship, aka the Hindenburg? Our good friend Jim was a volunteer guide at the museum, located at Love Field in Dallas.

**Captain Jim**

Jim is a storyteller extraordinaire who took us on a journey filled with fun stories and exciting adventures about the history of flight.

He guided us through the exploits of Leonardo da Vinci, the Wright Brothers, and twenty-first-century spacecraft, including a peek inside the Apollo 7 Command Module.

To add to the adventures, the girls could sit in the captain's chair in a Southwest 747 cockpit exhibit. This exhibit contains all the instruments and controls pilots use to fly from Dallas Love Field to anywhere in the world.

Check out the museums in your area. Many are interactive and provide an exciting and fun-filled experience.

## A Day at the Zoo

Sometimes, things don't go as planned. Going to the zoo in July in Dallas? We planned to get to the zoo early. After breakfast, leaving home with our sunglasses, sunscreen, and water bottles, we headed to the zoo. Never mind that it was going to be 100 degrees outside that day.

Because we were so early, we were able to find a parking spot right next to the zoo entrance. We realized that we would not have to fight the crowds today! As we began our tour, all the animals were lounging in the shade, trying to keep cool. Nothing was moving, not even a mouse!

It wasn't long before we found an artificial stream running through the zoo. It is a perfect place to remove our shoes and splash in the water to cool off.

Soon after that, we decided that our zoo day had come to an end. We needed to find a place to stop for ice cream and then go home to jump in the pool.

In other years, our visit to the zoo found that the animals were not lying in the shade resting but rather roaming around in their environments. Monkeys were playing and swinging from limb to limb, kangaroos were hopping around, and flamingos were standing on one leg in a cool pool. All in all, it was another fun day at the zoo.

When you plan your trip to the zoo, we have a couple of suggestions. On a hot day, a morning outing is best. The animals sit in the shade and nap if it is too hot. It's always fun to be at the zoo during feeding time. Many zoos have interactive exhibits that make the trip even more exciting.

## So Many Things to Do, So Little Time

As we continue this journey, we are constantly looking for new things around our city to include in the next year's adventure.

We try to mix up the activities for the week to provide variety and allow for free time at home. We also have alternatives in case we encounter a rainy day. When our granddaughters became tweens, we involved them in planning the week. More about that later.

While adventures are a big part of camp, it's our shared experiences with our granddaughters that build the bonds and memories we keep in our hearts. That is the joy we get from Grandma and Grandpa Camp each year.

*****

As you prepare for your version of Grandma and Grandpa Camp, relax with a glass of wine, a cup of coffee or tea, and think about all the adventures in your neighborhood and community that you could share with your grandchildren. Adventures can be as simple as going to the mall to ride the Merry-Go-Round or out for ice cream.

We are sure that you will find more adventures than you can possibly do in the time you have with them.

# CHAPTER 4

# NON-NEGOTIABLES

---

As time passes, some of the activities we do during Grandma and Grandpa Camp are requested to be repeated yearly. We try to have a nice variety of activities for the girls, but a few just become favorites. These are now 'Must Have' activities for each year. You will find certain activities that become favorites, and you will find a way to work them into your special time with your grandchildren.

## Afternoon Tea

Top among these is an afternoon tea that we have done for many years with the girls. In anticipation of the event, they pack their prettiest fancy dress to bring to camp. We all get dressed up, style our hair, put on makeup for the older ones, and get ready for the afternoon tea. Even Grandpa joins in and dresses up, sometimes in his tuxedo. The quiet, formal atmosphere, the tea sandwiches, the sweets, and various teas are all anticipated with great excitement. Even the youngest ones attend. On one occasion, the littlest one had her sippy cup next to her teacup!

Some tea rooms let them choose their tea, while others have tea pre-determined for every course. The girls take their places at the table, place their napkins in their laps, and await the presentation of the three-tiered plates and, of course, the tea, accompanied by sugar cubes and honey.

Their favorite tea room was Maudee's, owned by an older, very friendly couple. They took the time to explain the different teas, discuss tea trivia, and show the girls their teapot and teacup collection. The girls could choose several teas from those available and sample the tea sandwiches and sweets that are part of an afternoon tea.

The girls all loved going to Maudee's. However, one year, Mack and Sharon told us they were retiring and closing their shop. What a sad day that was for us!

Since then, we have been to several other tea rooms, but our favorite one now is at the Dallas Arboretum. Tea begins with a small cup of soup, followed by a tiered tray of cucumber, pimiento cheese, chicken salad, and other tea sandwiches. It ends with another tiered tray of sweet treats—scones, chocolate truffles, lemon tarts, and other sweets. A different tea accompanies each course. The girls' favorite tea is Stone Fruit Vanilla Rose.

**Afternoon tea**

There is a lot of sandwich trading when one likes something another does not care for, but all is done quietly and with good manners.

Before and after tea, we can also explore the beautiful Arboretum grounds and enjoy all the flowers, trees, and sculptures there.

**Arboretum**

The DeGolyer house, the original Spanish-style home on the Arboretum property, is on the grounds. We have toured the home a few times, and our favorite room is the library, which overlooks the lake and has secret closets.

Tea may not be the thing for your grandchildren, but they will discover an activity you do with them that they want to do again and again.

## Movie Night

Another favorite activity that is a part of camp every year is the Outdoor Movie Night. Uncle Sean has an extensive collection of movies, and we would pick a video and get it from him. Even though Uncle Sean does not have children, he has been a part of our Grandma and Grandpa Camp experience over the years. He has joined us on occasion for movie night, afternoon tea, and game night, enjoying time with his nieces.

In the earlier years, the girls helped Grandpa build the screen using 2x2s and a white sheet. They would then attach it to the fence, ready for the movie.

**Movie night prep**

Now, we have a portable projection screen that we set up each year, and the movies are streamed online. Sometimes the girls choose a video they have already seen, and other times they choose a new one.

Chairs are arranged on the lawn with small tables between them. We are set for the movie to start at dusk!

But how can you have a movie without food? In the kitchen, we put out a bowl of pizza dough, sauces, and lots of toppings. Each girl makes a small pizza, adding toppings and cheese to satisfy their taste.

Pizzas are put in the oven, popcorn is popped, and glasses are filled with their favorite drink. When the pizzas are ready, it is time for the movie to start,

After the pizzas are gone, it is time to go to the pool to continue to watch the movie. They love watching from the pool!

One year, when Alli, granddaughter number six, was the youngest of the group of campers, we thought she was too young to stay up that late, so we put her to bed before the movie started. Many years later, she told us she had woken up and watched from the bedroom window. She was not going to miss out.

**Movie time in the backyard**

What child doesn't enjoy going to a movie? It can be even more fun when it is in your backyard. Plus, it allows them to stay up late—what a treat!

You don't have to have a big backyard or a projector to have a fun movie night with the grandkids. Push back the furniture, throw a blanket and some pillows on the floor, and find a movie on the TV. Share some popcorn and pizza, and you are off to the races.

## Swimming

We are fortunate to have a pool in our backyard, so swimming in the pool is an activity that occurs every year—every day, in fact.

The non-swimmers had arm floaties, swim rings, and of course, Grandma and Grandpa close by. As time went on and they learned to swim, they would show what they had learned since the last time they were all together, and that presented a challenge to the others to keep up. Games were made up, and Grandma's feet were always tickled.

**Fun in the pool**

When additional granddaughters came to Grandma and Grandpa Camp for the first time, the older girls made sure to include them in the pool activities. They assisted us in helping the newcomers improve their swimming skills by floating on their backs, putting their faces in the water, and challenging them to swim short and longer distances.

Pool floats and noodles were used to stay afloat while not swimming.

Those good swimmers would do somersaults in the water, run and jump into the pool from the side, have races with their cousins, and even make up games to be played as they enjoyed the pool.

Occasionally, we would call them out of the pool, line them up against the wood fence, ask them to do fun poses and spray them with the hose. This would leave a dry silhouette of their form as temporary artwork on the fence.

Swimming at various times of the day also kept it fun. Sometimes, we would swim before breakfast, sometimes after dark, and sometimes they would be in and out of the pool and playing other yard games for the whole afternoon.

Occasionally, but not every year, we go to one of the local water parks so that they can go down the slides, float in the lazy river, and ride the waves in the wave pool.

Having fun in the water doesn't mean you have to have a pool in your backyard. Running through the sprinklers, splashing in a stock tank, jumping in and out of a small kiddie pool from Walmart, or spending an afternoon at a city pool, splash park, or a nearby beach are great opportunities to cool off on a hot summer day.

## Grocery Shopping

Groceries must be brought in to feed a large group for a week. Try as we might, we often did not go to the grocery store before they all started arriving. Grandma would sometimes be at the store as Grandpa was welcoming the campers.

However, as they grew old enough to help, it has become another fun activity to look forward to.

On the first day of Camp, Grandma and all the girls go to the grocery store together. The girls are divided into two teams, the list is split up, and they are off to find their assigned items (and sometimes more), bringing them all back to fill the cart to overflowing. Many texts go back and forth—what size, what brand, etc.

Last year, all four girls returned with cuddly stuffed animals that were a 'bargain' and asked with pleading eyes if they could get them. Grandma, being a softie, said yes.

## Game Night

We have always been a game-playing family, and camp is no different. The games vary yearly depending on the ages, whether we have new games, or whether the old standards are chosen for that year. Games are always available if anyone wants to play, but one night is designated as 'Game Night.' There have also been times when we played games over Zoom with distant cousins who could not attend in person.

**Game with cousins over Zoom**

We found an online Escape Room that we could play in with the Portland cousins. Dominos (a favorite to play with GGMa—their great-grandma), Wits and Wagers, Catch Phrase, Yahtzee, card games, and many others are among the games we've played.

Game night brings out the competitive streak in all of us, and lots of laughter.

## Camp T-shirts and Pictures

How do we keep track of all the campers when we are out in a group? We have Camp T-shirts! Not just any T-shirt, but one designed especially by the 'Artist of the Year.' Each year, one of the girls volunteers to draw the picture that will be printed on the shirt. Their creativity has led to many amazing pictures, each unique to the artist.

All the girls have had a couple of opportunities to be the artist for the year.

They send us a digital copy of their design, which we take to Big Frog in Plano, a custom T-shirt shop, to have printed on the shirts in a frame of sticks with "Grandma & Grandpa Camp" printed above the picture and the year printed below.

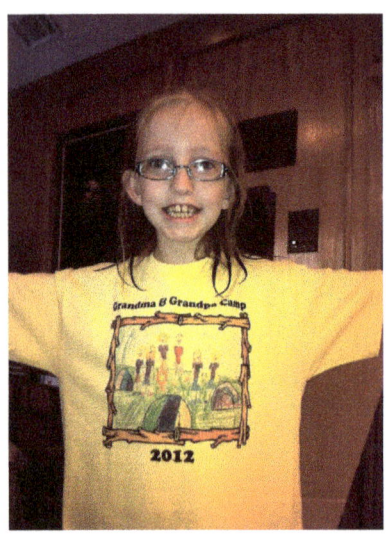

**Camp shirt**

As we go on our various outings, we introduce the 'Artist of the Year' if someone comments on the shirts. We all love the unique shirts. They are special memories of our week together.

The shirts are also used for our annual picture. Wouldn't you want to remember the campers each year? We certainly do. The photos are taken on Saturday while the shirts are still clean.

Of course, the photographers have many ideas about how we should pose. One year, they had motorcycle props for us. Another time, we took props representing what we planned to do during our week together.

After many years of pictures, the girls like to come up with new poses that they want to try out. Last year, they figured out how to spell the word "CAMP" with the letters shaped by their bodies. The photographers have as much fun as the kids, trying out different poses and combinations of the whole group—sisters, cousins, etc. What a fun way to start our week, with lots of smiles and giggles!

Picture day

\*\*\*\*\*

Our non-negotiables are things that our granddaughters look forward to every year. Over time, you will also identify some things that your grandchildren like to do repeatedly. Typically, we have found the non-negotiable activities are the ones where all ages can participate.

Watch for things your grandchildren enjoy doing repeatedly with you that may become your non-negotiable traditions.

# CHAPTER 5

# PLANNING THE WEEK

---

If you consider how you plan for your family vacation, you'll feel right at home as you see how we prepare for our week with our grandchildren.

## Set the Date Early

Setting the date for Grandma and Grandpa Camp well in advance is a crucial first step. The age of your grandchildren and the number of families involved will determine how early you need to start planning. This early planning is essential to avoid any scheduling conflicts.

Initially, it was easy for us to schedule this event on our calendar. At the time, we only had two granddaughters who were sisters, and their summer schedule was wide open. This would change as they got older.

Over time, the number of campers at Grandma and Grandpa Camp grew to include two more sisters and two cousins, for a total of six granddaughters from two families. Later on, two additional granddaughters could also participate in Grandma and Grandpa Camp, adding a third family to our consideration when determining the date.

As our granddaughters entered high school, finding a date that worked for everyone became more challenging due to conflicts with summer band, church camp, family vacations, and other commitments.

We usually start discussing with our granddaughters and their parents after the first of the year to finalize a date for our Grandma and Grandpa Camp. The process starts with phone calls to the parents and grandchildren to get the dates they are free in June, July, and August.

Every year, we get a calendar from our insurance man—you probably do, too. We use this calendar to block out the dates for family vacations, church camps, summer band, and any other summer commitments our grandchildren have. Once this is done, another call is made to choose a date for Grandma and Grandpa Camp from the open dates on the calendar.

Once the date is decided, we must confirm with the granddaughter who will design this year's camp shirt. As mentioned earlier, the camp shirt has become an essential component of our week-long camp.

## Medical Release Form

A medical release form and insurance information for each grandchild is vital to your preparation for Grandma and Grandpa Camp. While we hope never to use it, this form is a crucial tool in preparing for unexpected incidents. In our 25 years of hosting camp, we've only had to use the form once, when a suspicious bug bite required medical attention.

To get started, you can search the internet for a "Consent to Treat Minor Children" form. We have included a sample form in the appendix to help you gather the information you should have while your grandchildren are with you at your version of Grandma and Grandpa Camp.

## Planning the Week's Activities

Grandma and Grandpa Camp is not about babysitting. It's a golden opportunity for grandparents to immerse themselves in the joy of spending quality time with their grandchildren, to strengthen their bonds, and to create memories that will last a lifetime. As one of our oldest granddaughters recently said, "It's never too late to start." Whether for a day, a weekend, or a whole week, the sheer delight of sharing precious moments with your grandchildren will fill your heart with joy.

When our granddaughters were little, we went on a few outings, like taking a ride on the merry-go-round at the mall or going out for ice cream. Occasionally, something unexpected pops up that we can add to our schedule. We discovered a Disney-themed art exhibit and story time at a small gallery in Dallas, which was a delightful surprise during Grandma and Grandpa Camp that year. We even found a children's croquet set with two hoops and a chicken that laid an egg (ping pong ball) when hit in the chest, which was so much fun.

Each year, we look for new adventures and add them to the things we have done in the past to create an initial list of possible activities for this year's camp. Add the non-negotiables to the list, and we will have more than we can do during the week we are together.

**Planning the week**

As the girls grew older, we began to involve them in planning the activities for the week at camp. We would sit together at breakfast on the first morning of camp and review a list of possible activities and outings. During our first attempt at creating a list to present choices to them, we included several options such as trips to museums, a day in Fort Worth, lunch and a movie at Studio Movie Grill, attending a play, and so on.

To our surprise, the girls wanted to try to fit *all* the activities on the list into their schedule that year. We soon realized we needed to be more cautious and organized in our planning. The following year, we created a similar list but divided it into two columns: Column A and Column B. The girls were allowed to jointly choose two activities from Column A and three from Column B, in addition to the Non-Negotiables.

The following list is an example of activities in each group. Column A contains activities that are more expensive and thus need to be limited. Choices in Column B are less expensive or free, and are limited more by the time available during the grandchildren's stay.

| Grandma and Grandpa Camp Options for the Week | |
| --- | --- |
| A—Select 2 | B—Select 3 |
| Live Theater Performance | Science Museum |
| Ice Skating | Miniature Golf |
| Day in Ft Worth | Geocaching |
| Escape Room | Bowling |
| Lunch with Movie | Scavenger Hunt |
| Water Park | Picnic in the Park |
| Other | Fossil Hunt |
| | Cake Decorating |
| | Other |

In addition to the selections we have identified, there is room for other suggestions from the group to be included in our week's selections. There are always some negotiations among our granddaughters before the schedule is finalized. This method worked well, and we ensured everyone had a fun experience at camp.

## Time Together at Home

Remember to set aside some time to hang out with your grandchildren at home. Unstructured playtime and activities such as creating personalized accessories with duct tape or beads can also be a fun way for your grandchildren to bond and work together. Our favorite activities include a family game night and an at-home murder mystery dinner. Spending time together is important, as you will see later when we share the thoughts of our granddaughters.

## Updating Games and Craft Supplies

One of our usual stops is at the local pool store, where we look for games and toys to play with in the water. We usually get pool noodles, diving toys, and inflatable rafts to make our pool time more enjoyable.

We also stock up on arts and crafts supplies, which we can use during downtime. Over the years, we have collected coloring books and crayons, boxes of beads, multi-colored paper for drawing, rolls of colored duct tape, an origami guide, stickers, and other age-appropriate crafts to keep the girls entertained.

**Craft table**

## Creating Lasting Memories

Every year during Grandma and Grandpa Camp, we have the girls create a "Take Home" project that they can share with their parents about our adventures. In the past, our projects have included scrapbooks, posters, and journals. With the increasing use of cell phones, we have also started sharing photos taken during the week. Our granddaughters keep their scrapbooks on a shelf in their room to this day. Furthermore, we share our adventures with their parents, family, and friends on Facebook by posting several times during the week.

In preparation for a take home project, we added scrapbooks, glue sticks, stickers, decorative paper, and fancy-edged scissors to our supply list.

## Scheduling the Week

As our granddaughters grew older, we found it helpful to post a schedule of activities on the refrigerator. We're happy to share some of what we've done and incorporated into our routine. Here's an example of a schedule that you might find helpful:

| Saturday | Sunday | Monday | Tuesday | Wednesday | Thursday | Friday | Free Time Activities |
|---|---|---|---|---|---|---|---|
| Planning Meeting | Church | Walking Bridge downtown | Cake Decorating | T-Shirt Tie Dying | Trip to Fort Worth-Exchange Avenue & Bureau of Engraving | Trip to the garden shop to create a Fairy Garden | Swimming Playing Games Ice Cream Store Crafts Hanging Out Puzzles |
| Grocery Shopping | Perot Museum | Backyard Movie Night | Lunch with GGMa | Afternoon Tea | Free Time Activities | Fossil Hunting at the park | Dress up |
| Pictures | Free Time Activities | Free Time Activities | Murder Mystery Dinner | Game Night | | Getting Ready to Go Home | Take Home Projects Story Time Home Movies |
| Free Time Activities | | | Free Time Activities | Free Time Activities | Call home | Free Time Activities | |
| Meals | | | | | | | |
| Pesto Cream Pasta with Chicken | Magic Time Machine | Homemade pizza & Popcorn | Meatballs with Tortellini | Enchiladas | Taco Salad | Pocket Sandwich Theater | |

As you look at our sample schedule, you will notice that we attempt to schedule no more than two major activities in a single day.

- Saturday includes a grocery store shopping trip, picture day, a meeting with the girls to review the week's schedule, free time to settle in, and swimming.

- Sunday, we start the day by attending church with our granddaughters, then go home for lunch before heading out to the local science museum, which has interactive, hands-on exhibits. We finish the day with a fun dinner at the Magic Time Machine, a unique restaurant with servers dressed in costumes representing popular pop culture icons.

- Monday, we have a more relaxing day by taking a trip to run on the footbridge overlooking the Trinity River. Then, we'll be back home to swim and set up for our movie in the backyard.

- Tuesday is an at-home day with cake decorating and a Murder Mystery Dinner in our dining room.

- Wednesday morning is spent at home tie-dying T-shirts in the backyard. This is followed by an afternoon tea outing and then more time at home for game night to finish the day.

- Thursday is a day trip to Fort Worth to visit Exchange Avenue and tour the Bureau of Engraving. You will also notice that we have scheduled a call with their parents on Thursday evening. When they were younger, this was to remind our granddaughters that they would return home in two days.

- Friday is another day we spend close to home, building a Fairy Garden and later in the afternoon hunting for soft fossils. This is also when we prepare for the girls to return home.

In addition to the scheduled activities, we also make time to swim every day, and we have free time for play, crafts, and just hanging out. We also have unscheduled activities to fit in, like visiting the ice cream store and the park.

## Check List

Creating a checklist of tasks before camp begins is a good idea when planning for your own Grandma and Grandpa Camp. Over the years, we have developed a checklist that you can use as a reference to assist you in this process. It's important to note that not everything can be done at the last minute, and you may still miss something, but it's always good to relax and go with the flow.

Our checklist includes:

- Set date for Grandma and Grandpa Camp.
- Get a picture for the Camp Shirt from the "Artist of the Year".
- Update shirt sizes for all campers.
- Order Camp Shirts from Big Frog.
- Make an appointment for a group picture.
- Check craft and art supplies.
- Check pool toys and games.
- Check for what's new in town that could be included in your schedule.
- Create a schedule for the week, with options.
- Make an initial meal plan for the week.
- Create a grocery list.
- Get Medical Release and health insurance information from parents.

\*\*\*\*\*

While planning for your version of Grandma and Grandpa Camp, it is important to realize that this is just an outline of how you will spend time with your grandchildren. The plan should not be rigid, but one that allows for flexibility, free time, and taking advantage of the unexpected. Keep it simple, and remember that this is the time to enjoy their presence and create special memories you will share with your grandchildren.

# CHAPTER 6

# WHEN PLANS NEED TO BE FLEXIBLE

---

As anyone with children knows, you can plan all you want, but there are times that you must adapt and change to meet the current situation. Grandma and Grandpa Camp is no different.

The following stories are just some of the ways we adjusted our plans to meet the unexpected. As you will see, some were challenges to overcome, and others were pleasant surprises we could take advantage of.

## Scary Larry

Lindsey was about two, and her sister Ashley was four. They were the only two campers that year. As usual, we had taken a week's vacation and were excited to spend time with our two granddaughters.

The first day was filled with splashing in the pool, swinging on the tree swing, playing games, and taking a nap in the afternoon.

As the first day ended, it was time for a bedtime story, and with hugs all around, the girls were tucked in for the night. The lights were turned off except for a night light, so the room was not totally dark.

The first day was a success, and now it was time for Grandma and Grandpa to have some quiet time, or so we thought. Shortly after we closed the door to their bedroom, the girls came out and said they could not sleep because big eyes were looking at them, and they were scared! Big Eyes?

The closet in their bedroom has white French doors with two round brass doorknobs, the 'Big Eyes.' We had not anticipated this. It was time for bed. Houston, we have a problem. This is their room for the week! How can we make them feel safe in their bedroom? There must be something we can do. Do we take the doorknobs off the doors? Do we have another option?

We had an idea to take some copy paper, cover the closet doors, and cut out holes for the doorknobs. Next, we took a black Sharpie and drew freehand a large ugly face with a big runny nose, bushy eyebrows, a mouth with broken and missing teeth, big ears, and messy hair. The girls helped with the drawing, and "Scary Larry" was born. The problem was solved. This unexpected solution not only made the girls feel safe but also sparked a new tradition at our Grandma and Grandpa Camp for several years.

Sometimes, problem-solving can involve a bit of imagination and fun. Creativity goes a long way when dealing with the unexpected.

## I Wear Pink for Grandma

Another time we had to adapt was the year that Grandma was diagnosed with breast cancer (all is well now), and there was a possibility that surgery might be the same week as Camp.

I wear pink for Grandma

Since camp dates are determined far in advance, moving the date for the camp was not an option, and even as camp began, we still did not have a definite surgery date. The girls still wanted to come. They decided that if surgery did occur that week,

51

they would cook and take care of Grandma when she returned home from the hospital.

As in years past, we handed out the camp shirts on the first day of camp. To our surprise, the girls presented us with a second bag of shirts. These pink shirts said, 'I wear pink for Grandma.' It was very touching to feel their care and love. As it turned out, surgery was not until the next week, but they were prepared to take care of their Grandma in any case.

## Spur of the Moment

There are also times when we stumble across something that we can take advantage of. For example, we went to a local frozen yogurt shop. When we arrived, we discovered they offered free face painting for the children that day, so we waited our turn and took advantage of that opportunity. What a pleasant surprise!

**Face painting**

Another time, we went to see the Circus. Outside of the arena was a splash pool. After the Circus, our girls took their shoes off and joined many other little ones jumping and playing in the water to cool down.

It is important to keep your schedule flexible to take advantage of a fun but unexpected activity. Sometimes, the unexpected is more exciting than what was planned.

## Schedule Changes

In 2023, six girls joined us for Grandma and Grandpa Camp. However, two of our granddaughters, now college students, could only stay for the weekend. Working during their summer break provided funds for the next school year. But it was important to them to join their sisters and cousins for at least the weekend. Of course, we could not be happier that they wanted to come yet again to join us for Grandma and Grandpa Camp.

That meant we needed to change the schedule of activities for the week. The Friday night, Saturday, and Sunday schedules changed to include as many "Must Have" activities as we could squeeze into the weekend. A trip to the Dallas Arboretum for Afternoon Tea was moved to Sunday, and attending the melodrama at the Pocket Sandwich Theater was moved to Saturday evening. All the other prescheduled activities for the weekend remained unchanged.

## Zoom Calls with the Cousins

The two youngest cousins, Story and Colette, lived far away and could not attend camp in person during their early years. So again, we had to adapt. Each year, they got their shirts and even took part by drawing the picture when it was their turn. We sent the schedule of what we planned for the week so they could do similar activities at home.

Then, we discovered Zoom. While our remote campers could not participate in all of the onsite activities, we were able to utilize this platform to include them in many ways, including a talent show, game time, cookie breaks, and even an escape room. This not only allowed all the cousins to participate, but also fostered a sense of togetherness and fun despite the physical distance.

**Zoom call**

For the past few years, they have been able to come in person, which is *so* much better because we can spend the entire week together. However, using Zoom was still appreciated, as it allowed them to participate in Camp when they could not attend in person.

## The Pandemic

In 2020, COVID-19 significantly disrupted all plans for us. We told the girls we would have to skip this year because we could not go anywhere, but they had other plans! They were confident we could make it work, so they organized a Zoom meeting to discuss how that could happen.

We agreed that Grandma and Grandpa Camp was on for 2020, masks included. That summer, four girls from two families attended. We had to be creative because we were limited in what we could do, with so many places closed and restrictions on how many people could be together. So, we made the best of it and came up with ideas that could work.

We could still have the shirts made. Our camp shirt that year had pictures of eight viruses in a circle surrounding the phrase "Quarantine can't keep us from having fun," with the COVID virus as the 'o' in 'from.' Clever artist, Vanessa!

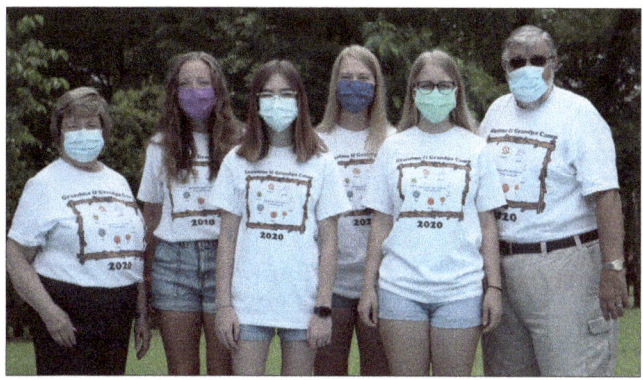

**Picture day at home**

No Picture Day meant taking candid pictures in our backyard and not visiting our friendly photographer at JC Penney.

We could not go out to restaurants, so we chose a 'Chef of the Day,' where one of the four girls was the chef, and the rest of us were her sous chefs as she made her favorite dinner. They each made up their menu—the entrees were Pesto Cream Pasta with Chicken, Meatballs and Tortellini, Enchiladas, and Baked Ziti. We ate well and had a lot of fun!

We gave them all some chalk, and they drew murals on the wood fence in the backyard. The artwork included a cactus garden, a house, a wave in the sunshine, and playing catch with a dog. Each was unique, and we enjoyed them for several weeks.

**Fence art**

Fossil Rim, the drive-through animal park, was still open, so we stayed in the car, safe from others, to view and feed the animals. We rolled up the windows quickly as the ostrich came near and pecked at them. Most of the animals ate food that we dropped on the ground from the car as instructed, but we were allowed to feed the giraffes from our hands. What a fun outing!

**Fossil Rim**

A scavenger hunt around the neighborhood was also fun for them. Touring the neighborhood in pairs and armed with their lists and cell phone cameras, they found the flamingos in a yard, the picket fence, a gazebo, the statue of a girl jumping rope, etc., taking pictures of what they found.

A cool drink was awaiting them when they returned.

Because we had many more at-home activities that year, the granddaughters in Portland were able to be more involved remotely. Since many of the girls play musical instruments, we had a talent show over Zoom, complete with a Master of Ceremony. Many games could be played on Zoom; we even scheduled a cookie break with the cousins.

Of course, the rules were still in place—no parents, swim every day, and have fun!

*****

**As you can see, adaptability is not just a necessity at Grandma and Grandpa Camp; it's a part of our family's DNA. The important thing is not to be rigid in your schedules but to enjoy your grandchildren and be flexible. When life throws you a curveball, take advantage of the opportunity! Adaptability is what makes our family camp so special.**

## CHAPTER 7

# WHEN YOUNG MINDS
# COME TOGETHER

F ree time is an important part of Grandma and Grandpa Camp. This is when the grandchildren's imagination kicks into gear, and young minds come together to dream up activities they can include in their week.

Through the years, games were invented, at-home tea parties were planned, a lemonade stand was set up, a strip mall was built out of construction paper, and even a zoo was built in one of the bedrooms, all while hanging out at home.

## Lemonade Stand

One year, the girls decided to have a lemonade stand on our street. But this was not your ordinary run-of-the-mill lemonade stand. This was a lemonade stand with a twist—it would also host an Art Fair, showcasing and selling the masterpieces they created earlier in the week.

With two festive tables, a pitcher of ice-cold lemonade, and their artwork carefully arranged, the girls were buzzing with anticipation. Their young, bright faces and biggest smiles were ready to welcome the neighborhood, eagerly awaiting their first customer.

**Lemonade stand**

Because our street is off the beaten path, they decided to set up when our neighbors would be coming home from work. While the sales were not brisk, we did have several neighbors stop by, and as luck would have it, a FedEx driver, who was delivering packages on our block, stopped to purchase a cold lemonade, perused the Art Fair, and bought a piece of art to take home. At the end of the day, the girls divided the cash to purchase souvenirs on our next outing. Needless to say, they were the talk of the neighborhood.

Remember, we talked about flexibility in our schedule. This was something our granddaughters came up with on their own. They planned it, created the artwork, prepared the lemonade, set up the tables at the end of the driveway, and made signs to advertise their enterprise. These budding entrepreneurs had an idea, created a plan, and worked as a team to make it happen.

## Cake Decorating

**The cakes are finished**

Bonding time with Grandma includes cake decorating. It all starts with a box of cake mix. It does not matter which brand or flavor, since the cakes are rarely eaten. Instead, they are just the canvas upon which masterpieces are created. The batter is prepared and placed in four small round white bowls called ramekins.

The cakes are placed in a 350-degree preheated oven. Twenty to thirty minutes later, they are removed from the oven and put on racks to cool, where they will stay until the next day. That is when the magic begins.

The girls embarked on their cake-decorating adventure with food coloring, sprinkles, marzipan, fondant, lots of frosting, and Grandma's cake-decorating kit ready. Like blank canvases, the cakes were transformed into pastoral scenes, modern art, seascapes, and more.

Their creativity went wild, and some beautiful, fun cakes were decorated. Pinterest was a big help in finding ideas. The cakes resembled a geode inspired by our trip to the Perot Museum gem exhibit, a bunny going into its burrow, a turtle swimming in a shimmering lake heading to the beach, a cookie monster, mosaics, and mirror-glazed cakes.

Pictures of the girls with their completed masterpieces were taken and put in the scrapbook for posterity.

## Free Time at Home

The kitchen table is the center of free-time activities at home. They can choose from all the craft supplies set out for their creative endeavors. Lots of creations are crafted.

The artist in them comes out when they draw pictures with crayons, colored pencils, or paints. Construction paper, foam letters and shapes, and stickers all contribute to their beautiful artwork.

**Being creative**

They love creating beautiful necklaces and bracelets with colorful beads and tiny rubber bands, and they proudly wear their creations all week long.

Designs are made using fusible beads on little pegboard shapes, then ironed to fuse the beads. Everyone had lots of these.

**Duct tape creations**

Duct tape creations included ball caps, cross-body handbags, and camera bags, using multiple colors and designs of duct tape to create unique fashion statements for this group of fashion-conscious young ladies.

These creations were included in the packet going home with them at the end of the week.

## Strip Mall

One morning, the girls took construction paper to create a strip mall. They designed logos for each store and added drawings to enhance the storefront. The construction paper was folded so each store stood erect on the floor. In the end, there were nine different storefronts and a small lake.

Their mall included a Chick-fil-A, a G&GC Dance Studio, a hospital, a vet clinic, an office building, the Perot Museum, which included origami dinosaurs roaming about, a Target store, Starbucks (one of Grandpa's favorite stops during Grandma and Grandpa Camp), a bank, and finally the Happy Smiles Dentist office. Are we looking at a group of future architects or discerning shoppers? Only time will tell.

Strip mall

## Ribbon Cutting Ceremony

We found an Origami for Beginners kit to include in our craft box. The girls created various birds and animals using the multicolored construction paper in the supply boxes. In fact, they made so many elephants, lions, tigers, and exotic animals that they decided to create a zoo to house these creatures.

They raided the closets to find enough shoe boxes for their project. Later that morning, we were invited to a ribbon-cutting ceremony for the grand opening of their Origami Zoo.

**Ribbon cutting**

I know that none of these girls belonged to a chamber of commerce and had never, to my knowledge, attended an actual ribbon-cutting ceremony. Yet, they had their own Grand Opening. The festivities included cutting a ribbon and pictures with the proud owners. The only thing missing was a press release.

## Tea Party in the Front Hall

The girls have always loved having at-home tea parties with dolls and stuffed animals. Our small round children's table with four stools and the Winnie the Pooh mini ceramic tea set is perfect for having tea with each other and their little guests.

**Tea party for two**

One day, a tea party was being hosted in the front hall. The menu included an assortment of cookies and other treats. We were presented with a special invitation to their restaurant for the tea party they were hosting.

Each girl had a specific role. One was the hostess, who greeted us at the entrance to the front hall, where the table and stools were set up, awaiting our arrival. Another was a waitress who presented the menu and took our orders. Others were cooks and servers who gathered little cookies from our cookie jar and juice from the refrigerator to fill our orders.

We were able to sit on the tiny stools—no small task, mind you—and enjoyed the juice and cookies with our granddaughters, adding to the memories we all shared about our time together.

## Take Home Projects

We look for creative ways for the girls to tell their stories so that they can share what they did at Camp with their parents. In the early days, we gave the girls disposable cameras so they could take their own pictures of the adventures we shared. Add in the scrapbooks, and we have a take-home project.

These scrapbooks contained photos, flyers, menus, and ticket stubs. Each was unique, with custom designed covers and notes about their time at Grandma and Grandpa Camp.

Later, we decided to change things up and replace the scrapbook with a poster. The supplies remained the same, except a 20x30-inch poster board replaced the scrapbook. The results were an amazing collage that told the story of our week together.

Memory Books are an excellent way for your grandchildren to recall their adventures at your version of Grandma and Grandpa Camp.

A few years ago, we learned about fairy gardens. So, with the help of our friendly gardener from Plants and Planters, our granddaughters created their fairy gardens.

Fairy gardens

The first task was to select the perfect container, which needed to be 12 to 14 inches in diameter and four to six inches deep to create their garden. Once the container was selected, with the addition of potting soil and the selection of just the right small plants or a patch of grass, the fairy garden began to take shape. But wait, there's more!

Next, they searched the shelves to select a small ceramic house, with accessories like a footbridge, a gnome, frogs, or mushrooms. The final touch was a package of small blue stones used to create a stream that flowed through their fairy gardens. All their treasures were attractively arranged to make each fairy garden unique. This was a fun project they could take home at the end of the week.

*****

**The unstructured time in our schedule allowed our granddaughters to be creative and work together on activities they dreamed up. These shared experiences have built strong bonds between them, so now they are not only cousins but also good friends.**

When you plan your version of Grandma and Grandpa Camp, be sure to include time that will allow your grandchildren's imagination to blossom. Sometimes, you can plant the seed and stand back to see what they do with it. Other times, they will come up with their own ideas. Either way, when young minds come together, amazing things can happen.

# CHAPTER 8

# FINDING ADVENTURES

We are often asked how we find so many adventures with our granddaughters at our annual Grandma and Grandpa Camp. For starters, we look for things we can do together. While we take some day trips to museums or the theater, the most cherished moments are the ones we spend together at home. Whether we're swimming, playing games, or working on projects, these times truly strengthen the bonds between us.

**Puzzle**

Board games, card games, puzzles, and outdoor games like bocce ball and croquet are not just games for us. They are opportunities for us to bond, laugh, and create lasting memories. These moments of shared joy and accomplishment are what make our Grandma and Grandpa Camp so special.

One of our favorite tips for finding treasures for the younger grandchildren is to look for gently used toys at neighborhood garage sales. We found the Fisher Price farm there. We also found the dress-up trunk at a church bazaar.

## Local Theaters

Over the years, we have found opportunities to support our local theater by attending live performances. Small community theaters can be a real bargain, with entertainment for all ages.

With four young girls in tow, we headed off to see a live performance of *Joseph and the Amazing Technicolor Dreamcoat* at the Dee and Charles Wyly Theater in downtown Dallas. It is a small theater where we were close to the action, with seats in the second row from the stage.

After the performance some actors returned to the stage to talk with the audience about the play. The youngest one in our group, who was four then, raised her hand and loudly proclaimed that she had enjoyed the whole movie. While we loved the play, this is the most cherished takeaway we still talk about all these years later.

Joseph and the Amazing Technicolor Dreamcoat

The Pocket Sandwich Theater is another fun place for families of all ages. It is a place to enjoy dinner and the thrill of a live theatrical performance in an intimate setting. These locally produced melodramas where the audience participates in the action, cheering on the hero or heroine, booing and throwing popcorn at the villain, and sometimes throwing popcorn at each other make an exciting night out.

**Pocket Sandwich Theater**

As the hero enters the stage, the music plays an upbeat melody to indicate that the good guy has arrived. In turn, the melody turns dramatic to signal the villain's arrival. All in good fun. After the performance, we got a picture with the actors to put in our scrapbooks.

As we were leaving, the girls told us that they wanted to arrive earlier next year to be sure to get a good seat close to the stage. To us, the most important part of that request was that the older girls were already planning to come next year!

Look for children's theater groups in your area. This is a great way to get your grandchildren to become part of the story, and it will be another fun-filled experience you can share with them.

## Community Resources

The internet is a great place to start looking for what is happening in your area that would be fun to do and available during the week of Camp.

Recently, we saw an ad on TV for a new museum in town, the Museum of Illusions. It is a unique museum with interactive experiences that challenge perception using optical illusions, visual tricks, and hands-on interactive displays to create a fun environment that engages us all. A new adventure was added to the schedule that year.

**Illusions**

## Tours

Our grandchildren are always interested in how things are made. We bet yours are too. A factory tour is always great fun. In Dallas, we visited the Mrs. Baird's Bakery. As we toured the plant, we walked along a long line of conveyor belts, moving dough through the factory into and out of large ovens, turning dough into bread. And the *smell* of freshly baked bread was outstanding!

Unfortunately, one granddaughter was too young to tour the facility, so she had one-on-one time with Grandma. They went to a nearby McDonald's to play in the playground. We met them in the store attached to the bread factory, where they found powdered sugar-covered donuts. All was not lost.

**Mrs Baird's Bakery tour**

As you've seen, it's crucial to be flexible in your plans, as restrictions can sometimes limit your ability to do things like a factory tour. Age, height, or other requirements can prevent one or more of your grandchildren from joining the tour. But fear not; there are always alternative activities to enjoy, ensuring everyone feels included and no one feels left out. If you cannot join a tour this time, note the restrictions and try again in the future when all your grandchildren can join in.

In Fort Worth, we toured the Bureau of Engraving, where we learned about printing money and the steps taken to prevent counterfeiting. If you decide to include this tour as one of your activities with your grandchildren, be sure to ask about the "star" dollars.

These are just some examples of the activities we found while checking out "What to do in DFW" websites.

Other opportunities you should consider are city parks, wildlife sanctuaries, minor league sporting events, and scavenger hunting in your city.

## Friends and Neighbors

As you look for adventures to include in your Grandma and Grandpa Camp, don't overlook the people you know who would love to share their interests with you and your grandchildren.

Our friend and neighbor Sandy, a talented artist who works with clay, spent a delightful afternoon with the girls, creating unique bowls, cups, and even a clay animal or two. The finishing touch was applying colorful glazes to these exceptional pieces.

Unlike Play-Doh, these creations were fired in her kiln. Once out of the kiln, they had to cool. At the end of the week, we returned to visit Sandy in her pottery shed and picked up the finished products. It was a wonderful opportunity to introduce our girls to a special friend who loved spending time with us and sharing her passion.

**Making pottery with Sandy**

Ruth, another close friend, introduced us to one of her friends who owns and operates a large cat rescue center in a nearby town. Visiting the center, we learned about its mission and how it treated and cared for the animals in its facility. It received animals from small roadside circuses where the animals had grown too old or had been hurt or neglected. In some cases, the animals were once small, cute pets that had grown too big or dangerous to keep.

We just happened to arrive shortly before feeding time, so we were able to observe how the animals interacted with the staff. Each animal had a story about how they were rescued. One animal from a local zoo had accidentally lost a leg and could no longer be part of their exhibit.

During our visit, we also talked with some students interning at the facility as part of their college degree program. Our final stop was a tour of the back wall, which is covered with memorial plaques in loving memory of the animals who had died at the center.

Another friend Tom, a pilot, took us to a flight school, where a flight instructor helped the girls fly a helicopter in their flight simulator. Tom also took us to visit the Southwest Airlines training facility to see where the pilots and flight crews train. During our tour, our youngest granddaughter, Colette, spotted a small rubber chicken hanging from a flight simulator model. As it turns out, when we got to the flight simulator area, we saw rubber chickens hanging on *all* the flight simulators.

**Flight school visit with Tom**

As the story goes, someone put a rubber chicken on one simulator, and the supervisor did not like it and had it taken off. Soon, there were technical issues with that flight simulator. The rubber chicken was once again attached to it. The problems were resolved, and as a result, a rubber chicken was attached to all the flight simulators for good luck.

Previously, we talked about our friend Jim, a volunteer at the Frontiers of Flight Museum at Love Field in Dallas, who led our personal tour. Our tour was filled with stories highlighting significant events in the history of aviation, including looking inside the Apollo 7 Command Module and sitting in the captain's seat in the cockpit of the 737 aircraft exhibit.

These experiences and more would not have happened without our friends and neighbors taking the time to share their passions with our granddaughters and us. You probably have such friends and neighbors as well. Invite them to share their passions with you and your grandchildren.

*****

We constantly learn from others who have their own version of Grandma and Grandpa Camp. Some spend time fishing in the afternoon with Grandpa or star gazing in the backyard, pointing out all the constellations as they move across the night sky, attending a minor league baseball game, and so much more.

Things are always happening around us, and we are always looking for new things to do. How often have you heard someone say that they have lived here their whole life but never took the time to visit a zoo, park, or notable landmark in their area? I am sure we all have said that at some time or other. Exploring places like these together with your grandchildren is simply the best. Don't be afraid to try new things!

# CHAPTER 9

# THOUGHTS FROM OUR
# GRANDDAUGHTERS

---

Four of our granddaughters grew up in Austin, Texas. Ashley and Lindsey are the oldest, and Grandma and Grandpa Camp began with them. Jenna and Vanessa joined their older sisters as soon as they were able.

Ainsley and her sister Alli live 30 minutes from our home in a neighboring community. They joined their cousins at camp when they were out of diapers, around the same time Jenna and Vanessa did.

Story and Colette, our youngest granddaughters, live in Portland, Oregon. In their early years, they joined in camp activities remotely. But more recently, they have been able to join their cousins in person.

Ashley and Lindsey are now married and living on the East Coast. Jenna, Vanessa, and Ainsley are college students balancing their academic responsibilities with their love for sports and friendly competitors during football season.

Alli and Story are high school students. Alli is a senior who will graduate this year, while Story is a freshman just beginning her high school career. Colette, our youngest granddaughter, is entering middle school this year.

As you read their stories, you will see how our granddaughters value their time at Grandma and Grandpa Camp and why they want that experience for their children when the time comes.

## Ashley

As the oldest grandchild, my experience with Grandma and Grandpa Camp surely changed the most over the years. When I was very young, I think the novelty of getting to stay in a different house for a whole week—with no parents! —was an exciting adventure in itself. My favorite activities had to be swimming every day—how fun to have a pool right in the backyard— and eating as much candy as I wanted out of the candy dishes that Grandma and Grandpa kept around the house.

It was great fun to play with different toys and any other objects we found around the house. Grandma's high heels, paperweights in the computer room, a decorative wagon with fake apples—the possibilities were endless.

In our elementary school years, my sister Lindsey and I became fast friends with our grandparents' neighbor's daughter, Michelle, who was around our age, and spent hours with her playing in the woods and the creek behind the neighborhood, climbing trees and hunting for treasure, or hosting tea parties with the dolls or stuffed animals of our choosing. Even better, the neighbors had a pool too, so we could double up our swimming time.

We started to appreciate exploring around the Dallas area with unique activities our grandparents found for us, like the Fort Worth stockyards, the children's museum and science museum, and even loved the simple things like a trip to Steak & Shake, since we didn't have those in our hometown. To this day I still get a little rush of adrenaline when I see a sign for Steak & Shake, thinking about that huge list of shake flavors!

In middle school and high school, we began to take on a new role as the "big cousins," as we were joined by our two younger sisters and two younger cousins.

Lindsey and I loved being big sisters, playing with and helping take care of our younger sisters, plus having even more little ones with our cousins around. I remember wishing I could have eleven siblings just like the family in *Cheaper by the Dozen*, so having cousins join the mix for a week was a step in the right direction for me.

Sometimes the Grandma and Grandpa Camp activities were targeted more toward a younger audience than for me and Lindsey, but then we got to show the younger ones the ropes and see them experiencing some of our favorite things for the first time.

We got to know our younger cousins much better through our time at camp together, whereas without this dedicated time together we might have seen ourselves as being more separate from the younger kids and not have as much opportunity for quality time with them.

Each year we saw them, along with our younger sisters, grow up from adorable toddlers into enthusiastic kids, and now into confident young adults. As we graduated from high school, we no longer had the ability to join Grandma and Grandpa Camp for a full week, due to summer internships and other activities, but usually still managed to carve out a special weekend to spend with our grandparents anyway before the other grandkids spent their week at camp.

Finally, our littlest cousins—15 to 18 years younger than me—started to join the camp too. Though we did not overlap with them in our Grandma and Grandpa Camp years, we saw the now-grown-up younger cousins get to form the same bonds with the littlest ones as we had with them in earlier years.

In this way, Grandma and Grandpa Camp forged bonds between the different "generations" of cousins through the time we spent together. To be able to spend days at a time in each other's company, making memories and having new experiences together, means that our cousins are really our friends, not just some relatives that we only see at the kids' table at Christmas dinner. (Though we do love to spend time together at the Christmas kids' table too!)

Equally important to our relationships with our cousins, Grandma and Grandpa Camp created a unique foundation for my relationship with my grandparents. Having time with them apart from my parents, starting at a young age, meant that my relationship with them was really my own independent relationship. They aren't just my parents' parents. They are my Grandma and Grandpa.

I wouldn't think twice about picking up the phone to call them and catch them up on how my week is going, same as any other close family member. I have a close and trusting relationship with them because they saw me grow up and invested time in me. They don't just know me through stories my parents told them, but through experiences we had together.

When my time at Grandma and Grandpa Camp was over, they found new ways to maintain our relationship as I became an adult. They visited me while I was in college out-of-state—and got their rental car stuck in the snow in the process—and stopped by for dinner whenever they were in town, once I moved back to Texas.

They know the small things still matter; they even call my husband for his birthday every year and sing the whole Happy Birthday song over the phone. They continue to commit to a close relationship and invest time in their grandkids' lives, but that foundation began because of Grandma and Grandpa Camp.

I think Grandma and Grandpa Camp is a wonderful tradition to pass down through the generations. What better way to create those special bonds between grandkids, grandparents, and cousins, especially for families that don't all live in the same city, than having dedicated time together to have fun?

Plus, from what I understand from my parents, it's pretty nice to offload the kids for a week and go take a nice vacation as a couple. This is an experience I would want my future kids to have, and for my parents and in-laws to build their own relationships with them.

# Lindsey

I have so many fond memories of Grandma and Grandpa Camp. From waiting impatiently until our parents left, to playing dress up with Ashley and Michelle, to swimming every day, there was no shortage of laughter and fun times.

I especially loved our yearly trip to high tea. We would dress up and have delicious teas and delicate pastries and sandwiches, and it always felt so grown-up and fancy. I think those years of high tea are where my current love of tea was born!

I also loved helping set up the makeshift movie screen for our outdoor movie, putting together 2x4s and attaching a sheet to them, then fixing the whole assembly to the fence. I'm not sure I ever contributed a meaningful amount to that building process, but I enjoyed being a part of it.

Things like that were a great way to have quality time with my grandparents, not just my sisters and cousins.

One way that we got that quality time was touring around Dallas. Each year, we had a few places that we would all go to get us out of the house.

We frequented an art museum for a few years, tried out other museums like the science museum, went to parks, visited statues, and more. One time, we went to an airplane museum where one of my grandparents' friends worked, and he had a ton of really specific and interesting information.

We would visit cool buildings and essentially act like tourists in Dallas. Sometimes, we would all wear our Grandma and Grandpa Camp T-shirts, which brought us more than a few comments and compliments.

Because these types of excursions were otherwise usually with our immediate families, it was a neat change of pace to explore a city with our grandparents and cousins. That gave each experience a more exciting and unique feel to it, even if we were going somewhere we'd gone before.

I loved getting to see more of the city where my grandparents lived, and it was a great way to add some variety in the schedule for the week. It was also a way to experience a different city in a way that would not normally have a reason to happen during larger family gatherings.

Every trip was a small adventure, led by Grandma and Grandpa, where we could learn something new or experience a new activity.

As a kid, I loved Grandma and Grandpa Camp for the lack of parents and regular house rules, adventures every day, and time to play with cousins. I still love the memories of Grandma and Grandpa Camp for all of those things, but as an adult, what I've come to understand is regardless of what activities we did at Grandma and Grandpa Camp, the entire experience every year was one more opportunity to build a relationship with my grandparents, my cousins, and my sisters.

Without Grandma and Grandpa Camp, every interaction with my grandparents as a child and growing up would have been through the lens of my parents—usually my parents and grandparents leading the conversation, not a lot of one-on-one time, and most activities would be group activities with the whole family.

Grandma and Grandpa Camp gave us a large chunk of time to build a foundation of personal relationship as grandparent and grandchild before I became an adult. It is much easier to foster and keep up that relationship now because we have shared joyful experiences and memories and set the precedent of spending time together without my parents.

The same is true for my relationship with my cousins. Living in different cities, we did not get a large amount of time to spend together while growing up, so getting that consistent time without large family gatherings to play and grow together was so precious. I think Grandma and Grandpa Camp even helped my relationship with my sisters, because it gave us a different environment in which to interact.

I think that Grandma and Grandpa Camp is an incredibly special experience, and I hope my parents will do the same for my future children. It's a great way to deepen family relationships and get to know each other on a much more personal level than you would normally get at a family gathering, especially if you live far from your grandparents.

It's a great week for everyone, even if it can be tiring: grandparents get to spend time with their grandchildren, get to know them and see them grow up in a more personal way; grandchildren love a week without parents and have a great time with grandparents and cousins, and get to see that their grandparents are pretty neat people; and parents can get a small vacation just to themselves, knowing that their parents and kids are getting a huge amount of value from their time together.

I would love it if my kids had a similar relationship with my parents as I do with my grandparents, and get to experience the unique things that come from spending a longer period of time alone with their grandparents.

I have so many treasured memories from Grandma and Grandpa Camp, from yearly traditions to one-time activities, relaxed time at the house to planned excursions around Dallas. Even if I don't remember specifics about each activity we did, the time spent together was well worth it. I can't recommend Grandma and Grandpa Camp enough!

## Jenna

I'm sure I am not the first to say this, but the thing that makes Grandma and Grandpa Camp special is not the activities we do, but the opportunities to spend time and develop relationships with both your grandparents and cousins. Especially as I have gotten older, I have appreciated how I am truly friends with my cousins, and I have a deep relationship with both of my grandparents.

When the grandkids were interviewed, most of us said that the unplanned downtime during the day was one of the most important parts of Grandma and Grandpa Camp. Between the bigger activities that Grandma and Grandpa had planned, we would have unstructured time at their house. Oftentimes, this would go longer than expected as one, or more often, both grandparents were running quite late for the thing we had planned later in the day.

When we were smaller, Grandma and Grandpa would have some potential activities for us to do during down time. Things like craft supplies, board games, and puzzles. There was one year where we made a bunch of origami and duct tape products and set up a lemonade and craft stand on the street.

Some of our favorite traditions came from things we started doing during this unstructured downtime—murder mystery dinners and decorating cakes. Downtime let us all rest (especially the grandparents) and gave us an amazing opportunity to become best friends with our cousins.

Unfortunately, an internship out of state means that my time at Grandma and Grandpa Camp has come to an end. I am so fortunate to have such loving grandparents who have welcomed me for the last 20 years. I will miss and cherish all the time I was able to spend with my grandparents and cousins.

## Vanessa

One of the things that I always look forward to is the Murder Mystery dinner. It's something that you can order online, or even at a bookstore. It comes with characters, scripts, clues, and, of course, the answer.

Grandma and Grandpa find a new one to do each year, and they all have different themes, settings, and characters. One of the traditions that we started to make it more fun was to dress up.

Each cousin and grandparent chooses a character that we want to be for that night. We raid the costume closet or Grandma's closet to make the most outrageous outfit. Every time, it is absolute chaos as everyone is running around trying to grab the clothes that most suit their character.

Of course, there are some negotiations that go on because someone has a shirt, pair of pants, or scarf that could work for more than one person. This is where using your imagination is important, because it is rare that all four cousins can make the best possible outfit.

This past year, we managed to pull together four pretty good outfits. Colette used Grandma or Grandpa's tan pants, Grandma's blue jacket, a hat and scarf that she found, two koala bear stuffed animals, and a belt to bring to life her zookeeper character.

Alli used her white skirt, black tank top, a pearl necklace that she found in a box, and a white flower clip to portray a rich woman.

Story wore flower pants, a bright orange shirt, tied a red blanket around her waist, put a bandana around her head, and wore a red scarf and a couple of necklaces that she found. She also had a deck of cards in her hand, which really tied the tarot card reader look all together.

I put on one of my shirts with the craziest design on the front, found a pink pom-pom and used it as a wig, got two boas and put one around my neck and the other around my waist, put blush on my nose to make it look red, and found a broken pair of fairy wings in the back of a closet to finish off my mute clown look.

Even though I am now 18, having this one night to dress up and solve a murder brings me and my cousins so much joy and laughter. The whole evening is very unserious, but it is always fun to experience the twists and turns of the story until, eventually, the killer is revealed.

Whether it was Grandpa reading aloud that he was the killer when we were not even halfway through the game, or everyone attempting to do some kind of accent to get into character more, this night has always been a part of my most cherished memories with my cousins and grandparents.

Going to Grandma and Grandpa Camp gave me unique opportunities like that to bond with my cousins. I stay up late talking to them almost every time we see each other, and I love being able to support them whenever I can.

We also have gotten close to our grandparents. They came up to visit me at college and I really enjoyed seeing them. If we hadn't had that isolated time to connect, I would not be as comfortable around them as I am today.

I want my kids to have the same experience. I'm always excited to go to my grandparents' house, and I love seeing my cousins. I've made so many amazing memories at Grandma and Grandpa Camp, and I hope that my kids feel the same way about their grandparents and cousins.

# Ainsley

Grandma and Grandpa Camp has been one of the highlights of my life for as long as I can remember. I know so many people who only talk to their cousins or grandparents a couple of times a year on holidays, and I realize how extremely lucky I am to have had Grandma and Grandpa Camp.

Not only do I get to hang out with my cousins and grandparents for a week straight each year, but the relationships that week fosters are much stronger than most anyone else's are with their extended family.

During the actual week of camp, tea is easily one of my favorite activities. It's one of our most tried and true traditions, and we haven't missed a year. When I was little, I was the pickiest eater and would rarely step out of my comfort zone when it came to food. Tea was not only a fun time, but I also really learned to diversify my palate and try new foods and teas.

I have always loved getting dressed up for any occasion, but this one always holds a special place in my heart. Going to tea is different than just going out to eat—it's a whole experience. And getting to do that all growing up is a luxury that I'm so grateful for and will truly never forget.

I grew up about a 30-minute drive away from my grandparents, but unfortunately didn't get to see them as much as I would've liked or probably should have. Grandma and Grandpa Camp, however, helps us become so much closer just because of the quality time we spend together, the jokes we make, and the love we all share.

My grandparents came and visited me at college because we have a relationship where they can do that. I think that is pretty rare, and I am so happy I was blessed with this family.

I know I am also lucky that I am pretty much the direct middle child between all of my cousins. There are two older, two younger, and four in the middle. The middle girls I went to camp with for the longest time were a year older and a year younger than me, so we always had so much in common, especially the older we got. Now, the three of us are all in college and still talk pretty often, especially during football season when we trash-talk each other's schools relentlessly. Roll Tide!

My little sister is also part of that middle group. We have always gotten along, but not always been the closest of sisters. Luckily, we have incredible parents who always push us to have a good relationship. I believe camp really fostered and developed that relationship so that now, we are very close and text or call daily.

I still maintain great relationships with my oldest and youngest cousins. The oldest two always showed up for me. They were examples for me to look up to as the oldest child. I really needed people like that in my life, and am so grateful that I had them growing up, and still have them going into adulthood.

The youngest two started coming to camp toward the end of my time, but I am still able to have a close relationship with them. I know how much I looked up to my older cousins as role models, and I always want to be that for them as much as possible.

Ever since I was little, I've known that this is something I want for my future kids, for my kids' sake but also for selfish reasons. I have amazing parents and a very good relationship with my sister, and I know my parents will be amazing grandparents when that time comes.

Obviously, I've had a great time at Grandma and Grandpa Camp, so there's no doubt in my mind that my children will love it, too. But also, my parents have always talked about how they love getting a little break, and that it gives them an excuse to see my mom's siblings who she's also super close to. I know my parents have loved seeing our connections with our family grow over the years.

If you have the opportunity, *please* send your kids or host Grandma and Grandpa Camp. I've created countless lifelong memories and have developed deep connections with my whole family, all because of one week per year.

## Alli

Without question, the part of Grandma and Grandpa Camp I look forward to the most is getting to see my cousins.

Getting to spend a week together every summer since I can remember has made us so close. That week, we get to catch up on everything that has been happening since last year in each of our lives. I absolutely love tea, and movie night, and all of our other activities and traditions, but the part of Grandma and Grandpa Camp I look forward to the most is the midnight conversations while getting ready for bed, and catching up on lost time.

The first night of Camp is always fun for the cousins. Even before we start the activities, we stay up talking and letting the time fly by. Some of my core memories of Camp are sitting on the counter and talking until we remembered that we had to wake up early in the morning and decided to call it a night.

The late-night talking has brought us so close, and that doesn't go away during the remainder of the year. Grandma and Grandpa Camp gives us proximity and time, but we all talk to each other regularly. I know that if I ever needed anything, I could call any of my cousins and they would be there to help or support me however they can.

In fact, I call Jenna or Vanessa probably at least once a month to help me with physics or calculus homework. But while we can call with things that we need, we also just regularly call to hang out and catch up, like friends do.

I think Grandma and Grandpa Camp has also made my sister and me a lot closer. Even when we lived in the same house, we didn't always get to hang out and just talk. My sister is my best friend (hi Ains!), and I'm not sure if things would be that way without the time we spent together at Camp.

Camp has also let us become really close to our grandparents. Not a lot of kids get to spend a week with just their extended family, catching up and making countless inside jokes. We are so lucky to have grandparents who care to be involved in our lives and want to have a relationship with us. That is more impactful for us than even they might realize.

Even though we didn't always get along when we were younger, those things just brought us closer. As we grew up, became more responsible, and learned more, we could put those old disagreements behind us. That's the beauty of getting together every year. We learn and grow together, and we all generally become better people together.

I wouldn't trade Grandma and Grandpa Camp for the world. The bonds, the random inside jokes (Operation Midnight Macaroni might have failed, but it lives on forever in our hearts), so much laughter and joy, and years of traditions. I wish every kid got to experience Grandma and Grandpa Camp. I am so lucky to have such an amazing family, and a big part of the reason we are so close and connected is because we have bonded so much over the years, which affects the entire family dynamic. The week itself is so incredibly fun, and the impact that it makes is so strong.

# Story

If you asked me what my favorite part of summer was, I would probably mention road trips, traveling, and the fresh, sweet air. But one thing I would not fail to mention is Grandma and Grandpa Camp. Everything about Grandma and Grandpa Camp is such an amazing experience: going to tea at the Arboretum, seeing our cousins, watching movies, playing games, traveling around Texas, and most importantly, the quality time making good memories.

We of course have our own special and meaningful traditions—which you can start with your families too—but every year there are so many new things to do that being bored isn't even a possibility. Every moment we spend together is an adventure that I will cherish for the rest of my life.

Though there are so many great things that we do, one of my favorites has to be movie night. Almost nothing beats setting up a projector in the backyard, pizza in hand, in the dusky warmth of July with the people you love, then relaxing in the pool until the sun has set way below the horizon. No matter how other people would want to do movie night, it's always such a great time. We all know no one is really there just for the movie.

Of course, we always do movie night in the pool, all together, which is one of the best parts, in my opinion. It's especially relaxing after a day full of activities to be able to just float and have fun during the movie. We watch different movies each year and always have a great time. Even setting up the projector itself creates memories that no one will forget.

However, coming to Grandma and Grandpa Camp at all is always important to me, movie night or not. It had always been a wish of mine when I was younger. Since we live so far away, it felt like it would be so much fun to arrive in town once a year to spend a week of quality time with my cousins and grandparents. My sister and I had always wanted to go, but by the time we were allowed to spend the week away, we had to join virtually due to COVID—from Oregon to Texas!

Though engaging virtually definitely wasn't the same as being there with your family, as you get to be there for the activities but not the downtime where the most important memories are made, it was a great way to keep us connected. Now that we can come in person, it's been a very important experience to us.

We had always been close to our cousins, but as extended family, now we are more like best friends, and that connection has changed our family so much for the better.

In the future, when I am much older and have a family of my own, I would be thrilled if my parents put on their own Grandma and Grandpa camp.

Though my sister and I are younger than our other cousins and struggled with the pandemic once we were old enough to come, it has become one of the highlights of the past few summers. I remember as a younger child being jealous of my cousins who got to go. Now that I come as well, I realize I was right to be.

If my kids were able to have the same incredible experience that I've had, that would mean the world to me. Grandma and Grandpa Camp is all about building strong, unbreakable bonds with your family - making everyone closer to each other than before every year - and those strong relationships are exactly what I would want my family to have.

## Colette

Grandma and Grandpa Camp is more than just a camp. It is a time to connect with your family, build relationships, learn who your cousins truly are, learn about your grandparents, and have fun.

A few of my favorite activities include high tea, murder mystery dinners, and generally spare time with cousins. Tea is a time to wear fancy dresses, look at flowers in the Arboretum, trade sandwiches and desserts, and, of course, drink tea. Murder mystery dinners are a time to put our heads together, dress up, and laugh. And hanging out with cousins is a time to laugh even harder.

But right now, I'm going to talk to you about Fort Worth. Fort Worth is yet another place fit for memories with family. We have bought cowboy hats, gone to the cowgirl museum, and my sister and I have even ridden a longhorn.

You walk through the old brick roads with spirits high and enjoy stopping somewhere heavily air-conditioned because Dallas gets really hot in the summer, and there is little shade there.

Horse-drawn carriages clop all over the streets, and you may see a cattle or two on the sidewalk. Someone may ask for a few dollars for you to sit on one, so come prepared.

The Cowgirl Museum is a large building with paintings, outfits, and even areas for you to virtually design your own boots. All in all, Fort

Worth is a place to explore and soak in the scenery of the Wild West around you. Get riding, cowgirl/boy!

*****

You have just read the thoughts of our granddaughters about how Grandma and Grandpa Camp impacted their relationship with us and each other. They want to continue this family tradition when they become parents. Like us, they too hope you can find some way to create a similar family tradition for your family.

# CHAPTER 10

## PARENTS SHARE THEIR THOUGHTS

As you have read, we have eight granddaughters from three families: one in the Austin area with four daughters, one in the greater Dallas area with two daughters, and one in the Portland area with two daughters.

The following comments are from the parents, sharing their thoughts about the impact of Grandma and Grandpa Camp on their family.

## Karen and Mike

The first Grandma and Grandpa Camp started as a chance for my parents to spend time with our children. We lived 200 miles away, and whenever we would visit, we had a great time, but had to squeeze in visits with several different family members, and there wasn't a lot of downtime. So, when our second daughter was around nine months old, my parents gave us a gift that I don't think we were allowed to refuse.

"When you wean Lindsey, we'd like to take the kids for a week, and you can go away." I was conflicted. I had never left my children overnight, much less for a week, but the thought of a vacation without them was amazing. Mike had no qualms and made reservations for a cruise to take me far enough away that I couldn't go back until the week was over.

We dropped off the girls with a two-page list of directions, precautions, preferences, and schedules. A woman who has known me since birth was sitting at the table as I reviewed the list with my mom, waiting patiently for me to finish before commenting, "You know your mom has raised four children and can do this, right?"

I looked deep into her eyes and responded, "You could be Jesus, and I would still have to give you this list."

I knew she didn't need it. I did. And with that, I could leave my children in my parents' very capable and loving hands.

We walked into our cabin to start the cruise and found a bottle of wine and a note saying, "Have a great time! Love, Mom and Dad," and I burst into tears. Not a promising start to the week. But not long after, we were standing in the sunshine on a deck overlooking the water, looking forward to the time we could focus on each other, have uninterrupted conversations, and sit at a dinner table where there was only solid food.

I finally got to call on Wednesday, and the girls yelled hello as they were running by the phone playing chase. They were having so much fun they hardly noticed we were gone. The rest of our trip was wonderful.

In future years, we would alternate taking a couple's vacation and staying at home to see friends and work on projects. It was the perfect time to clean out old toys, clothes, and crafts. Every two years, I took out a five-foot diameter, three-foot-high pile of trash that they never even noticed was gone.

One year, when we stayed home, we had several friends over for a dinner party early in the week. As we were sitting down to eat, someone asked, "Do you miss the kids?"

Mike and I looked at each other, and to our mutual surprise, replied in unison, "No!"

On Saturday, we would be counting down the minutes until they returned, happy and full of stories to share, but on Tuesday, we were fully enjoying the uninterrupted adult conversation and the security of knowing that our children were having the time of their lives.

Coming home wasn't always a seamless event, however. It took a little while to remember that Mom and Dad Rules are different from Grandma and Grandpa Rules, that candy is only a food group at their house, and then there was the time that we did the end of camp handoff in Waco when the girls were in the middle of watching ET. They ran to our car, eager to continue the movie as we drove them the rest of the way home, and (spoiler alert) three minutes into the drive, ET went home. Our sobbing children could hardly be consoled, and they have not watched that movie again to this day—almost twenty years later!

Slowly but surely, summer internships and college courses bring Grandma and Grandpa Camp to an end for our girls, but it's a sweet and gradual process as they reduce their time to a long weekend, a few "Big Kid" days, and finally, an occasional facetime call to check in on the younger ones.

In reality, it will never truly end. We are looking forward to keeping this cherished tradition alive with our own grandchildren when they come, carrying on my parents' legacy of creating beautiful memories and deepening the love in our extended family that knows no generational boundaries.

# Jennifer and Mark

Unlike her siblings, Jennifer's family has always lived about 30 minutes from her parents. The thing you need to know about Rosemary and Mike, aka Grandma and Grandpa, is that they are very social beings. They have always had a very busy calendar between work and social obligations. So just because we lived closer to them did not mean we saw them as often as you might imagine.

Jennifer's sister, Karen, had children a few years before we did, which meant we got to watch Grandma and Grandpa Camp as the "cool aunt and uncle" while the first two kids attended it. Once we had our own kids, we were very excited to send them to camp. We knew our girls would have a blast and we would get some much-needed sleep and lots of date nights. But honestly, we never could have imagined how big of a win-win-win this one week a year would become.

Right from the start it was obvious that the first huge "win" was simply the time the cousins spent together and the bonds they developed.

Our two girls and Karen's two younger girls grew up going to Grandma and Grandpa Camp, with the four of them all together. Every year the cousins would challenge each other to learn something new during that week. The challenges could be anything from swimming without holding your nose, to being the most creative, to cooking difficult recipes.

Once the girls got into middle school and they all had cell phones, they created a group chat that would get used extensively during Camp week, and also occasionally throughout the year. Once the older two were in high school, that group chat became very active all year round. They chat with each other about all kinds of stuff, like good friends do.

When our oldest daughter, Ainsley, was touring universities trying to figure out which school would become the setting for the next chapter of her life, her first call upon making her big decision wasn't to her mother, as one might expect. No, her first call was to her cousin, Jenna, who was super excited for her.

When Karen's youngest, Vanessa, went off to college, our youngest, Alli, would have long facetime calls with her to check out how her first year was.

The four of these girls have said many times that they will be good friends for the rest of their lives.

Jennifer's brother, Brian, has two daughters who are a bit younger than ours and live across the country. When Brian's girls were able to come to camp in person, the four middle cousins cleared their schedules so they could attend that whole week. They wanted Brian's girls to have the best camp possible, and they knew the cousin factor mattered!

So the "win" of the tight bonds between the cousins is one of the wonderful and unexpected things that came out of Grandma and Grandpa Camp.

The second "win" from Grandma and Grandpa Camp is the relationship our girls now have with their grandparents. Our girls have a relationship with Grandma and Grandpa that is completely their own and no longer relies on us to drive it. Both our girls will call their grandparents just to catch up because they have not seen them lately. It is not uncommon for us to find out about something going on in Grandma and Grandpa's lives from one of our kids who had just called them to catch up.

When Ainsley went to college nine hours away, Grandma and Grandpa went to visit her for a weekend. Ainsley loved it, took them everywhere, and introduced them to all her friends. So now when they talk on the phone about what's going on at school, Grandma and Grandpa have a first-hand frame of reference for the places and people in Ainsley's life. All three of them had a ball that weekend.

When Alli turned 16, she wanted a tea party for her birthday. She did not talk to Jen, her mother, to plan that party. She called her grandparents. Tea parties are an annual signature event at every Grandma and Grandpa Camp, so Alli knew that Grandma and Grandpa would understand what she was thinking for the party. Even better, Alli asked if they would host it at their house. The three of them were thick as thieves planning the menu, the time, and the various teas. We were only brought in when it was time to go to the store to buy the supplies. Our girls have no hesitation in calling their grandparents for things like this, and we love it!

It is so easy to inadvertently foster a second-hand relationship when kids only spend occasional and sporadic time with their grandparents. We are grateful for the strong, direct relationship our daughters have with their grandparents. It is one of the wonderful and magical "wins" that came from Grandma and Grandpa Camp.

The third "win" from Grandma and Grandpa Camp was, a bit selfishly, the reconnection time we got to have while our kids were away for a week each summer.

The traditional "opening ceremony" of Grandma and Grandpa Camp involved us dropping off the girls, and then the girls giving us cursory hugs and ushering us away so they could begin the festivities we weren't invited to, as we were frequently reminded! We would play along and act all sad as they shooed us out the door, telling them we would call every hour to see how much they missed us. And then we would high-five as we drove away, knowing we had a week to ourselves!

We tended to stay in town during that week. There were nightly date nights, catching up with friends we maybe didn't see as often, and sleeping the glorious sleep of people who don't have busy kid logistics to manage during the day. But mainly the week was about reconnection with each other.

The other great thing about Grandma and Grandpa Camp week was getting to clean out kid closets, toy chests, stuffed animal bins, and craft bins without kids all of a sudden remembering how much they loved that random toy they had not played with in two years. They always came home and marveled at how great their rooms looked. And most of the time they had no idea anything was missing! We kept the toys and stuffed animals in a hidden "temporary holding area" just to make sure we didn't accidentally toss something they truly loved but never talked about.

The friends we hung out with during Grandma and Grandpa Camp week always knew where our kids were, and everyone always begged to let their kids attend. They knew how much our kids loved to go, and they also saw how much we would be refreshed by the time the kids came home. The refreshing and reconnection was certainly the third "win" of this amazing tradition.

We all knew we were blessed to have this week every summer. But I don't think I could have understood what the lasting effect this week would have on each of us.

# Brian

Since we have lived more than two thousand miles from Dallas since my daughters were born, their first experiences with Grandma and Grandpa Camp were virtual, where they participated in a talent show with their cousins and did some crafts over zoom calls. They of course loved these interactions, but a few years ago, we booked a flight to Dallas so the girls could participate in person for the first time.

They were so excited to go, even though this was going to be their first night away from home without either parent with them. The week went off without a hitch. No tearful calls from homesick campers, just quick check-ins to let me know they were having fun and to say goodnight.

On the flight home, they showed me their scrapbooks, which chronicled their time at camp, and were so happy and appreciative to have been able to spend this quality time with their extended family. My parents had run a pretty amazing week, filled with tours of local attractions, melodramatic theater, and visits to fun themed restaurants.

But when I asked the girls what they enjoyed most from their time at Grandma and Grandpa Camp, none of these made the list. What they really valued most was the time they got to spend engaging with each other—playtime with the cousins, movie night in the backyard, relaxing in the pool, dressing up in character, and having a Murder Mystery night in the dining room.

They absolutely loved it, and I felt so thankful that they were able to strengthen those family bonds and recognize the value of those relationships in their lives. I am also deeply grateful that my parents took the initiative to create such a loving and caring space to nurture these relationships.

Ever since their first in-person experience, Grandma and Grandpa Camp has been a top summer priority in our family. It's quite literally the best thing going, and I hope we'll be able to continue for several years to come.

*****

Parents can get a week off from parenting by simply sending their children to summer camp, band camp, scout camp ... you name it. So why is Grandma and Grandpa Camp any different?

First, it is a time for sisters and cousins to spend time together away from home in a safe and loving environment with their grandparents. The second benefit is not so obvious. They also develop a relationship with their aunts and uncles.

When we have the entire clan together, there is plenty of fun and good-natured banter between the nieces and their aunts and uncles as dinner is prepared. Once the meal is finished, the table is cleared and the game is on. It is a fun time to be together playing a game that all ages can participate in.

Now that our granddaughters are attending different universities, the family chat on game day is filled with comments and commentary from the sisters, cousins, aunts and uncles, and even the grandparents. Grandma and Grandpa Camp has not only built bonds between our grandchildren and us, but the bond has also expanded to include strong relationships within the entire extended family.

# CHAPTER 11

# OUR STORY CONTINUES

**Grandma and Grandpa Camp 2022**

As we shared stories and pictures of our Grandma and Grandpa Camp with our friends, many showed great interest in doing their own Camp. There are different names—Nana and Papa Camp, Grammy and Granddad Camp, Grandparent Camp - anything that makes sense for the grandparents and grandchildren.

We have also spoken to others with similar family experiences, sometimes with the parents included, sometimes one-on-one with their grandchild, and sometimes taking a mini vacation together.

Just as we are excited to share our stories about our time with our grandchildren, so it is with all the grandparents we know. We get ideas from others that help improve our time with our granddaughters. For example, we took the idea of including a camp shirt that each of us would wear during Grandma and Grandpa Camp from a conversation with another grandparent over coffee.

We never anticipated how strong our relationship with our granddaughters would become, or the joy we'd experience when we are together as a result of our Grandma and Grandpa Camp. You see, it's not just about the grandchildren; it's about the relationships you are building with them. Grandma and Grandpa Camp is a win for you, too!

We have shared many of our experiences with you, but there are more to come. We are already working on the next Grandma and Grandpa Camp.

We hope you can take some of these ideas and run with them to create your own special time with your grandchildren. As every relationship is unique, your camp with your grandchildren will be unique, too.

What will your Grandma and Grandpa Camp look like? Start by setting a date that works for everyone and planning activities that cater to your grandchildren's interests. As they get older, involving them in decision-making can make them feel more excited and invested.

Whether it's a night, a weekend, or a week, this is your time to actively engage with your grandchildren. Going on an outing, playing games, having a karaoke night, or looking at family photos with them are simple ways to start.

If you can start when they are young, you have lots of time to make memories and build bonds. But if they are older, as our granddaughter Ashley said, "It's never too late to start." Young or old, they will look forward to coming year after year.

Remember, the important thing is to be together sharing experiences with your grandchildren!

There is no magic formula, but *magic will happen* when you share your time and experiences with your grandchildren.

# APPENDIX

We have included a sample "Consent to Treat Minor Children Form" for use in the event of an unexpected medical emergency that requires a visit to the doctor or emergency room for a grandchild in your care.

Additionally, you'll find a Camp Activity Planning Worksheet to help you organize and plan activities for your version of Grandma and Grandpa Camp. This worksheet is designed to help you brainstorm potential activities and refine them into a final camp schedule.

To further help with your planning, we've provided a Sample Camp Schedule as a guide in creating your own. You can even post it on your refrigerator for quick reference.

Lastly, we've compiled a few more helpful planning tools, including a Camp Prep Checklist outlining tasks to consider early in the planning process, a Tour Checklist to help determine if a tour is a good fit for your grandchildren at this time,  a list of 10 useful internet searches, and a list of local resources and possible places to visit to help you discover activities in your community.

# CONSENT TO TREAT MINOR CHILDREN
## Please print all information

I, _____, parent or legal guardian _____,
born _____, do hereby consent to any medical care and the
administration of anesthesia determined by a physician to be necessary for the
welfare of my child while said child is under the care of _____
and I am not reasonably available by telephone to give consent.

This authorization is effective from _____ to _____

_____

Signature of Parent or Legal Guardian

_____            _____

Witness Signature                            Witness Name (please print)

> **This consent form should be taken with the child to the hospital or physician 's office when the child is taken for treatment.**

This additional information will assist in treatment if it can be furnished with the
consent but is not required.

Family address _____

Telephone: Father _____ home _____ work

Mother _____ home _____ work

Child's Birthdate _____ Last Tetanus _____

Allergies to drugs or foods _____

Special Medications, Blood Type or Pertinent Information

_____

_____

Child's Physician _____ Phone _____

Insurance _____ Policy # _____

Preferred Hospital _____

## Camp Activity Planning Worksheet

| Activity | Day | Notes |
|---|---|---|
| | | |
| | | |
| | | |
| | | |
| | | |
| | | |
| | | |
| | | |
| | | |
| | | |
| | | |
| | | |
| | | |
| | | |
| | | |
| | | |
| | | |
| | | |
| | | |
| | | |
| | | |

Use this template to list all the activities you can think of. Include ideas from your grandchildren as well. Then narrow the list to create your camp schedule.

## Sample Camp Schedule

| | Saturday | Sunday | Monday | Tuesday | Wednesday | Thursday | Friday | Free Time Activities |
|---|---|---|---|---|---|---|---|---|
| | Planning Meeting | Church | Walking Bridge downtown | Cake Decorating | T-Shirt Tie Dying | Trip to Fort Worth-Exchange Avenue & Bureau of Engraving | Trip to the garden shop to create a Fairy Garden | Swimming Playing Games Ice Cream Store Crafts |
| | Grocery Shopping Pictures | Perot Museum | Backyard Movie Night | Lunch with GGMa | Afternoon Tea | | Fossil Hunting at the park | Hanging Out Puzzles Dress up |
| | | | | Murder Mystery Dinner | Game Night | Free Time Activities | Getting Ready to Go Home | Take Home Projects Story Time Home Movies |
| | Free Time Activities | Free Time Activities | Free Time Activities | Free Time Activities | Free Time Activities | Call home | Free Time Activities | |
| Meals | Pesto Cream Pasta with Chicken | Magic Time Machine | Homemade pizza & Popcorn | Meatballs with Tortellini | Enchiladas | Taco Salad | Pocket Sandwich Theater | |

**It is important to remember that the schedule is not carved in stone. Be open to taking advantage of the unexpected adventure.**

## Camp Prep Checklist:

- Set date for Grandma and Grandpa Camp.
- Get a picture for the Camp Shirt from the "Artist of the Year".
- Update shirt sizes for all campers.
- Order Camp Shirts
- Make an appointment for a group picture.
- Check craft and art supplies.
- Check pool toys and games.
- Check for what's new in town that could be included in your schedule.
- Create a schedule for the week, with options.
- Make an initial meal plan for the week.
- Create a grocery list.
- Get Medical Release and health insurance information from parents.

## Tour Checklist:

- Tour name: _____
- Address: _____
- Contact: _____
- Phone: _____
- Dates(s) tour available: _____
- Start time(s): _____
- Tour length: _____
- Tour restrictions:
  - Age _____
  - Height _____
  - Other _____
- Admission fee: _____
- Self-guided tour: Yes/No
- Handicap accommodations: Yes/No/N.A.

## 10 Useful Internet Searches:

1. Things to do in _____ (your city/town)
2. Scavenger hunt in _____ (your city/town)
3. Fun activities for kids
4. Host a murder-mystery dinner for kids
5. Duct tape projects
6. Free coloring pages for kids
7. Origami for beginners
8. Outdoor fun for kids
9. Cooking with kids
10. Crafts with supplies at home

## Helpful Resources and Local Treasures:

- Brochures for local attractions can be found in hotel lobbies
- For a list of tours in your area visit the local Chamber of Commerce
- Inquire about Story Time for Children at your local library
- Explore local community theater groups for family productions
- Check out free community band concerts in the park
- Spend an afternoon at the movies
- And don't overlook a picnic in the park

# ACKNOWLEDGEMENTS

We extend our heartfelt gratitude to our wonderful granddaughters—Ashley, Lindsey, Jenna, Vanessa, Ainsley, Alli, Story, and Colette—for sharing their lives with us and sharing their thoughts and experiences about Grandma and Grandpa Camp included in this book.

A special thank you to our children, Karen and Mike, Jennifer and Mark, and Brian, for their insights and support throughout this incredible journey with their children.

We are deeply grateful to our son Sean and Cris for generously sharing their love for their nieces and their extensive movie library, making our movie nights even more special.

Our sincere appreciation goes to our alpha readers, Charlie Maubach, Karen May, and Carol Hewitt, whose invaluable feedback helped shape our manuscript.

A special thanks to Debbie Mrazek—Nana, business executive, and friend—for taking time from her busy schedule to write the foreword for our story.

We would also like to recognize our dear friends who generously shared their talents and passions with our granddaughters:

- Sandy Kettelhut, for welcoming our granddaughters into her pottery shed, where they created cherished treasures.

- Jim Masal, our forever Captain, for igniting their interest in aviation history as the Captain of the Hindenburg at the Frontiers of Flight Museum.
- Tom Allen, for sharing his passion for flying by arranging exclusive tours at the National Training Center for Southwest Airlines and the Helicopter Institute, where our granddaughters had the thrilling opportunity to fly a helicopter in a flight simulator used to train future pilots.
- Ruth DeSario, for introducing us to the founder of In Sync Exotics, a nonprofit dedicated to rescuing and caring for injured and mistreated exotic cats.
- Joe Mock from Big Frog Custom T-Shirts and More, who has been printing our camp shirts since 2012, adding a personal touch to our cherished memories.

Thanks to Sami Ali, caricature artist at Magic Time Machine, for creating the caricatures of our granddaughters.

We truly appreciate the encouragement and support from Karen Pina, Katelynn Koontz, and TJ Marquis from Selfpublishing in helping us share our story.

Lastly, our deepest gratitude goes to our family and friends for their unwavering encouragement and support, inspiring us to share the story of Grandma and Grandpa Camp.

www.ingramcontent.com/pod-product-compliance
Lightning Source LLC
Chambersburg PA
CBHW051214120626
46547CB00013B/1345